V. SACKVILLE-WEST

V. Sackville-West in her writing room in the tower at Sissinghurst, 1938. The photographs on her table are of Virginia Woolf and the Brontë sisters.

V. SACKVILLE-WEST

A CRITICAL BIOGRAPHY

Michael Stevens

CHARLES SCRIBNER'S SONS

NEW YORK

Contents

Illustrations

Foreword

V. SACKVILLE-WEST IS AN AUTHOR WHO does not yet appear to have received the attention that her work merits, for although her novels, biographies, and poetry are widely read, little seems to have been written about her since her death in 1962. While in no way claiming that the present critical biography is complete, or even does justice to the complex personality or works of this interesting writer, it is my hope that it will contribute some information and insight which may stimulate some later biographer to write the fuller work on her which she deserves.

I should like to take this opportunity of acknowledging the debt of thanks I owe to all those who have been of assistance to me while writing this biography. My greatest debt is to Nigel Nicolson, without whose unstinted aid from the very first, this work could never have been written. His generosity in placing his mother's manuscripts and other papers at my disposal, in indicating other sources, some of which, unfortunately, are not yet available, and in answering so many questions, has been invaluable.

I am also indebted to Dr. Marianne Beyer, who has followed the development of this book since its inception, to Patricia Cristol for invaluable help with the American edition, and to several of my colleagues for comment and advice. Last, but by no means least, my thanks to my wife and daughter for their patience and understanding.

Major Works

YEAR	V S-W'S AGE	POETRY	FICTION	NON-FICTION
1926	34			*Passenger to Teheran*
1926	34	*The Land*		
1927	35			*Aphra Behn*
1928	36			*Twelve Days*
1929	37	*King's Daughter*		
1929	37			*Andrew Marvell*
1930	38		*The Edwardians*	
1931	39		*All Passion Spent*	
1931	39	*Sissinghurst*		
1932	40		*Family History*	
1932	40		*Thirty Clocks Strike the Hour*	
1933	41	*Collected Poems*		
1934	42		*The Dark Island*	
1936	44			*St. Joan of Arc*
1937	45			*Pepita*
1938	46	*Solitude*		
1941	49	*Selected Poems*		
1942	50		*Grand Canyon*	
1943	51			*The Eagle and the Dove*
1945	53	*Another World Than This (with H.N.)*		
1946	54	*The Garden*		
1947	55		*Devil at Westease*	
1953	61		*The Easter Party*	
1959	67			*Daughter of France*
1961	69		*No Signposts in the Sea*	

Chronology

June 1913	The lawsuit to contest Sir John's will.
July 1913	The engagement between V S-W and Harold Nicolson made public.
1 Oct. 1913	V S-W and Harold Nicolson married at Knole.
Oct. 1913	Honeymoon in Italy and Egypt.
Winter 1914	The Nicolsons in Constantinople.
June 1914	Return to England.
Aug. 1914	Birth of Benedict Nicolson at Knole.
Oct. 1914	The Nicolsons move to London.
1915	*Constantinople* privately published.
Summer 1915	The Nicolsons purchase Long Barn, near Knole.
Jan. 1917	Birth of Nigel Nicolson in London.
1917	*Poems of West and East.*
May 1918	Beginning of affair between V S-W and Violet Keppel (Trefusis).
1919	*Heritage.* Harold Nicolson at the Peace Conference in Paris.
Feb. 1920	V S-W elopes with Violet Trefusis to Amiens. Crisis in marriage of V S-W and Harold Nicolson.
1921	*The Dragon in Shallow Waters. Orchard and Vineyard.*
1922	*The Heir. Knole and the Sackvilles.* First meeting with Leonard and Virginia Woolf.
1923	*The Diary of Lady Anne Clifford. Grey Wethers. Challenge.* A start made on *The Land.*
1924	*Seducers in Ecuador,* written for Virginia Woolf.
1925	The bulk of *The Land* written.
Feb. 1926	V S-W goes to Persia, returning in the summer via Russia.
Autumn 1926	*The Land. Passenger to Teheran.*
1927	V S-W returns to Persia and makes a journey through the Bakhtiari Mountains. H.N. transferred to Berlin. V S-W awarded the Hawthornden Prize for *The Land. Aphra Behn.*
Feb. 1928	Death of Lord Sackville. Knole passes to V S-W's uncle.
1928	*Twelve Days.* Virginia Woolf publishes *Orlando.*
Autumn 1928	V S-W and Virginia Woolf on a trip in France.
1929	*King's Daughter. Andrew Marvell.* Harold Nicolson receives an offer from Lord Beaverbrook and hands in his resignation to the Foreign Office. He moves into chambers in the City.
Jan. 1930	Harold Nicolson joins the staff of the *Evening Standard.*

May 1930	The Nicolsons buy Sissinghurst Castle in Kent. *The Edwardians.*
1930	*Sissinghurst.*
March 1931	Harold Nicolson joins Mosley's New Party.
May 1931	*All Passion Spent.*
August 1931	Harold Nicolson resigns from the *Evening Standard* to edit *Action.*
Summer 1932	Harold Nicolson leaves the New Party and starts reviewing.
Oct. 1932	*Family History. Thirty Clocks Strike the Hour.*
Jan. 1933	The Nicolsons leave for a three-month lecture tour of the United States.
Autumn 1933	*Collected Poems.*
Spring 1934	V S-W and Gwen St. Aubyn in Portofino, then, with Harold Nicolson, in Morocco.
Oct. 1934	*The Dark Island.*
April 1935	The Nicolsons on a cruise to Greece.
Autumn 1935	V S-W in Domrémy, Chinon, and Orleans to do research for *Saint Joan of Arc,* accompanied by Gwen St. Aubyn.
Nov. 1935	Harold Nicolson elected M.P. for West Leicester.
Jan. 1936	Lady Sackville dies.
May 1936	*Saint Joan of Arc.*
1937	Tour of North Africa. *Pepita.* Jorney with Gwen St. Aubyn to France.
1938	*Solitude.*
March 1941	Virginia Woolf commits suicide.
1942	*Grand Canyon.*
1943	*The Eagle and the Dove.* V S-W passes through a spiritual crisis.
1946	*The Garden.*
Jan. 1947	V S-W makes a start on *Daughter of France.*
Feb. 1947	Harold Nicolson joins the Labour Party.
June 1947	V S-W awarded the Heinemann Prize for *The Garden.*
1947	*Nursery Rhymes. Devil at Westease.*
Dec. 1947	V S-W made a Companion of Honour.
Feb. 1948	V S-W goes to North Africa for two months to lecture for the British Council.
March 1948	Harold Nicolson defeated in a by-election.
March 1949	V S-W goes to Spain on a lecture tour for the British Council.
1949	Becomes a Justice of the Peace, sits on the National

	Trust's Gardens Committee and the Executive of the Society for the Preservation of Rural Kent.
Dec. 1950	V S-W starts writing *The Easter Party*.
Jan. 1953	*The Easter Party*.
March 1953	Work resumed on *Daughter of France*.
March 1955	V S-W injures her back.
Dec. 1955	Steegmuller publishes his biography of La Grande Mademoiselle.
Jan. 1957	The Nicolsons on a cruise to Java.
Dec. 1957	On a cruise to South America.
Autumn 1958	*Daughter of France* finished.
Jan. 1959	Cruise to Singapore and Saigon. *No Signposts in the Sea* begun.
March 1959	*Daughter of France* published.
Summer 1959	V S-W ill with virus pneumonia.
Jan. 1960	Cruise to South Africa. Bulk of the work on *No Signposts in the Sea* done.
Summer 1960	V S-W ill.
Jan. 1961	Cruise to South America. *Faces* written.
Feb. 1961	*No Signposts in the Sea* published.
Jan. 1962	V S-W has a hemorrhage. Cruise to the West Indies.
March 1962	Cancer diagnosed.
2 June 1962	V S-W dies at Sissinghurst.

CHAPTER I

❦ Ancestry ❦

VICTORIA SACKVILLE-WEST'S ANCESTRY IS somewhat unusual. On her father's side she is descended direct from Thomas Sackville, 1536–1608, later Lord Buckhurst and 1st Earl of Dorset. On her mother's side she is descended from a Spanish gypsy known as Pepita.

As a young man, Thomas Sackville made a reputation for himself as a poet—his contemporary, John Heywood, complimented him:

> There Sackville's sonnets sweetly sauced
> And featly finèd be.

Today he is better remembered as the writer of the *Induction* to the *Mirror for Magistrates* and the *Complaint to Buckingham,* and as the co-author of *Gorboduc.* At the age of thirty, however, Thomas Sackville, who was cousin to Queen Elizabeth through the Boleyn family, abandoned poetry for politics for which, by birth and by talent, he was eminently fitted. In the course of the next thirty years he was knighted, created Lord Buckhurst, of Buckhurst in Sussex, appointed Lord Chancellor of Oxford University, and, in 1599, was made Lord High Treasurer of England. After the death of Queen Elizabeth, he was confirmed in his office by James I, who elevated him to an Earldom as Earl Dorset in 1604.

Apart from Thomas Sackville's poetic gifts, there are two other facts about him which are of importance when considering the life and works of V. Sackville-West (henceforth referred to as V S-W): in 1554 he married Cicely, daughter to Sir John Baker of Sissinghurst

Castle in Kent, and in 1556 Queen Elizabeth presented him with Knole, one of the great country houses of England and, even at that time, a building of some magnificence and fame.

During the reign of George I, Lionel Cranfield Sackville, 7th Earl of Dorset, was created 1st Duke of Dorset, but the title was destined to die out in less than a hundred years. When the 4th Duke of Dorset died in 1815 at the age of only twenty-one, a distant cousin succeeded to the title as 5th and last Duke. Knole, however, with all its revenues, remained the property of the Dowager Duchess, passing after her death into the hands of her daughter, Lady Elizabeth Sackville. Lady Elizabeth had married in 1813 John West, 5th Earl de la Warr, by whom she had nine children: six sons and three daughters. The second and third sons, Charles and Reginald Sackville-West, succeeded to their father's title, becoming the 6th and 7th Earls de la Warr. The 4th son, however, Mortimer Sackville-West, was created 1st Baron Sackville in 1876 and inherited Knole. The fifth son, Lionel Sackville-West, V S-W's grandfather, was to inherit both the title and Knole upon the death of his brother in 1888.

Lionel Sackville-West cannot have been the conventional man he looked. A diplomat by profession, he was noted for his taciturnity; indeed, toward the end of his life "he was . . . a queer and silent old man. . . . He turned his back on all visitors, but sized them up after they had gone in one shrewd and sarcastic phrase."

Yet in 1852, while on leave in Paris, he met and immediately fell in love with a twenty-two-year-old Spanish gypsy dancer known as Pepita, whose life-story V S-W was later to write in the book of the same name.

Pepita, or to give her her real name, Josefa Duran y Ortega de la Oliva, is said to have been a strikingly beautiful girl for whom her ambitious mother, Catalina Ortega, had arranged dancing lessons with a view to getting her an engagement at the Teatro del Príncipe in Madrid, at that time the leading theatre in Spain. The dancing lessons were a failure and Pepita's contract was canceled, but one of the male dancers at the theatre, Juan Antonio de la Oliva, had fallen violently in love with her and canceled his own contract with the theatre in protest. On 10th January, 1851, Pepita and Oliva were married, but only three months later, probably as the result of a quarrel with Catalina Ortega, Oliva walked out of the house, leaving his wife forever. Pepita left Spain shortly afterwards and went to northern Europe, where, within a few months, she had made a name for herself as a Spanish

Lionel Sackville-West, second Lord Sackville, 1881.

Josefa Duran y Ortega de la Oliva.

dancer in Denmark, France, and, in particular, in Germany as "The Star of Andalusia."

From 1852, the year in which Lionel Sackville-West and Pepita first met, until 1871, when Pepita died, they lived together although they could not, of course, marry as Pepita was a Catholic and could not have obtained a divorce even if she had tried. Sackville-West's career took him all over Europe, and Pepita continued to dance until the birth of their third child in 1865, so they had to set up house in many towns: in Heidelberg, Hackenberg, Turin, Como, and in Bordeaux. In 1865 she settled down in a house in Arcachon, where she spent the rest of her life. She died in 1871 giving birth to a stillborn son.

The problem now arose as to what was to be done with the five surviving children—two boys and three girls. Sackville-West himself obviously could not look after them, particularly as he was posted to Buenos Aires as British Minister shortly after Pepita's death. A temporary solution was found when a friend of Pepita's, Mme. de Béon, moved into their house and looked after them there. Then, in 1873, the eldest daughter, Victoria Josefa Dolores Catalina, V S-W's mother, was sent to a convent school in Paris, where she spent the following seven years. She was later joined there by her younger sisters.

In 1880, when Victoria was eighteen, all the children with the exception of Maximilian, the elder son, who had been established as a farmer in South Africa, were suddenly transported to England through the offices of Mas Mulhall, a woman whom Lionel Sackville-West had met in Buenos Aires. There Victoria discovered that Lord de la Warr and Lord Sackville were her uncles, and that the Duchess of Bedford and the Countess of Derby were her aunts. The Countess of Derby perceived that in Victoria there was material for something quite different from the governess for which she had been trained at the convent. As her brother, Lionel Sackville-West, had just been appointed British Minister in Washington, she determined to use her influence to send his illegitimate daughter with him as his hostess and mistress of his household. Though the suggestion caused consternation at first, both in British and in American circles, all opposition to the idea eventually collapsed, and in 1881 Victoria sailed for America to take charge of her father's household.

She appears to have been an immediate success, for although—or perhaps partly because—she could speak English only imperfectly, and because of the great charm and beauty that she is said to have

Victoria Josefa Dolores Catalina, Lady Sackville, 1900.

possessed, she had all Washington at her feet. It is reported that President Arthur himself made a proposal of marriage to her shortly after her arrival. She refused all suitors, however, continuing to look after her father's household until, in 1888, a disaster overtook him. During the presidential election campaign of that year he was incautious enough to reply indiscreetly to a letter, purporting to come from a Mr. Charles F. Murchison, which requested his views on the merits of the presidential candidates. The letter·was published in the daily press, and the resulting public excitement was made the pretext by the American Secretary of State for declaring Sackville-West *persona non grata*.

By a strange coincidence, however, his brother, Mortimer, 1st Baron Sackville, died three weeks later, thus offering Lionel Sackville-West an opportunity of giving up his career and returning to Knole in order to administer the estate to which, with the title, he had suddenly succeeded. He was offered another important diplomatic post by Lord Salisbury, but refused it.

After a few months spent in France while certain legal complications were being cleared up, Victoria took over the management of Knole for her father. She was at the time being courted by a young French marquis, but though apparently attracted by him, she evidently felt that she could hardly leave her father to look after Knole by himself. Just at this time of indecision she met her cousin, Lionel Sackville-West, who was also the heir to the title and to Knole. He fell violently in love with her and asked her to marry him. Faced with the choice of becoming either a French marquise or an English peeress (with Knole), she eventually chose the latter; she and her cousin were married at Knole a year later, on 17th June, 1890.

CHAPTER II

❧ 1892–1913 ❧

THE EARLY MARRIED LIFE of the young Sackville-Wests appears to have been very happy. They were very much in love and they had plenty to occupy themselves with. Until his death in 1908 Lord Sackville was nominally head of the household at Knole, but in fact he took no part in running it, devoting himself entirely to his own interests. Victoria, his daughter, assumed full responsibility for the house itself, and Lionel, his nephew and heir, attended to the business of the estate as well as to his responsibilities as commander of the West Kent Yeomanry and his position on numerous committees in the County of Kent.

The characters of Lionel and Victoria were, however, completely different. V S-W has described her father as "the best type of English country gentleman; just, courteous, and conscientious, he was truly loved and respected by all."

Victoria, on the other hand, was mercurial in the extreme. In V S-W's own words:

> My mother was adorable at that time of her life. She was tiresome, of course, and wayward, and capricious, and thoroughly spoilt; but her charm and real inward gaiety enabled her to carry it all off. One forgave her everything when one heard her laugh and saw how frankly she was enjoying herself. As a child can be maddening at one moment and irresistible the next, so could my mother be maddening and irresistible by turns. For, like a child, she neither analysed nor controlled her moods: they simply blew across her.

7

And again:

> Many people have told me what a clever woman my mother was,
> and what good taste she had; it was a sort of label tied onto her;
> but it was utterly wrong. She was anything but clever, and her
> taste was anything but good. What they never realised was that
> she was, above all things, herself. Wrong or right, tiresome, trou-
> blesome, turbulent, difficult, generous, mean, vindictive,
> revengeful, unjust, kind, lavish, enthusiastic, all in turn, she was
> always herself, and to be always oneself to that extent is a form of
> genius.

It is clear that in a marriage between two such fundamentally dis-
similar personalities an open breach must come sooner or later. It was
the 1914–18 war that was responsible for the final disruption. Until
then they had divided their mandates at Knole fairly amicably, but
while Lionel, who had succeeded to the title by that time, was away in
the Middle East and France, the only check on Lady Sackville's always
autocratic character was removed, and she grew used to holding un-
disputed sway over the whole of Knole. When her husband returned
after the war, he made it clear to her that he intended to resume control of the estate, and the resultant clash of wills led to their final separation. Lady Sackville left Knole in 1919 and went to Brighton, where
she had a house. She never returned to her husband.

Victoria's charm and the fascination she held for other people
are evident throughout the whole of the second part of *Pepita.* One of
the people to fall permanently under her spell was Sir John Murray
Scott, whom she had met for the first time about 1900. Sir John, who
was destined to become an integral part of the Sackville-West family
until his death in 1912, must have been a remarkable man. Of middle-
class Scottish origin, he had become secretary to Sir Richard and Lady
Wallace, heirs to the property of the Marquises of Hertford and
owners of the vast collection of art that is now the property of the nation—the Wallace Collection. Sir Richard and Lady Wallace had
grown so fond of Sir John that they had made him their heir, and on
their death he inherited not only about a million pounds in cash, but
also the Wallace-Hertford properties in Paris—an enormous apartment in the Boulevard des Italiens filled with art treasures—and
Marie Antionette's Bagatelle in the Bois de Boulogne. Sir John seems
to have succumbed to Lady Sackville's charm at their very first meeting, and although they were to have many violent quarrels in the

Lord and Lady Sackville, at Knole, 1911.

Sir John Murray Scott.

years that followed, he never failed to return to her within a short time. He was frequently at Knole, and the Sackville-Wests regularly spent long periods with him in Paris or in Scotland.

In 1908 Lord Sackville died, and immediately a threat that had been hanging over the heads of Victoria and Lionel Sackville-West since 1896 became a reality. Victoria's brother, Henri, had claimed that Pepita's marriage to Juan Oliva was not valid and that Lionel Sackville-West (Henri and Victoria's father) had married Pepita in secret, thus making his children legitimate and Henri the rightful heir to Knole and the title. Investigations in Spain had revealed that someone had tampered with the entry in the register of the church in which Pepita and Oliva had been married, and Henri had been doing everything in his power to procure evidence to show that Lionel Sackville-West had married her. Quite naturally, the press was not slow to make the most of the lawsuit that followed the death of Lord Sackville, particularly as it was necessary for Victoria to establish the fact that she was illegitimate to make it possible for her husband to succeed to the title, and for about a fortnight the Sackville-Wests lived in a blaze of publicity. Eventually, Henri's case collapsed in court, and Victoria and Lionel Sackville-West returned to Knole in triumph as the rightful Lord and Lady Sackville.

Two years later, in 1912, Sir John Murray Scott died, leaving to Lady Sackville a legacy of one hundred and fifty thousand pounds plus the entire contents of his apartment in Paris, valued at over a quarter of a million pounds. His relatives were furious and decided to contest the will on the grounds that Lady Sackville had exercised undue influence over him. Coming as it did only a short time after the sensational lawsuit to determine the inheritance to the title, the press did not fail to exploit the case to the full. Lady Sackville was not the person to compromise by trying to obtain a settlement out of court, and after a brilliant defense in which eminent counsel were involved on both sides, she won her case.

It was to these parents that V S-W was born at Knole on the 9th of March, 1892, and it was against this background that she grew up until her marriage in 1913.

Her mother (who, to avoid confusion with V S-W, will henceforth be referred to as Lady Sackville, although she did not come into the title until 1908) appears not to have been a motherly woman by temperament, but even if she had been, her responsibilities as hostess at Knole and the Edwardian conception of how children of the aristocracy should be brought up would have prevented her from being in very close touch with her daughter. As it was, the first ten or twelve years of V S-W's life do not seem to have been remarkable for the close contact between mother and daughter. According to V S-W:

> She loved me when I was a baby, but I don't think she cared much for me as a child, nor do I blame her. My principal recollection of her then is that I used to be taken to her room to be "passed" before going down to luncheon on party days, when I had had my hair crimped; and I was always wrong and miserable.

And again:

> I can't remember much about my childhood, except that I had very long legs and very straight hair, over which Mother used to hurt my feelings and say she could not bear to look at me because I was so ugly.

V S-W was an only child, and Lady Sackville seems to have made no secret of the fact that she would never have any brothers or sisters, for V S-W notes that "she says she would have drowned herself sooner than have another child."

Frequently V S-W had to spend considerable periods alone at Knole with her grandfather when her parents were away on visits. Old Lord Sackville, who was then nearly eighty, was strange company for a young and sensitive girl. He was eccentric and morose, although he liked children and had many little private jokes with V S-W. Her recollection of him was as being

> very old, and queer, and silent. He hated people, and never spoke to the people who came to the house; in fact, if he got the chance he used to go to London for the day when he knew people were coming, and I used to be left alone to entertain them.

And further:

> Of all human beings, he was surely the most inscrutable. I lived with him for sixteen years, and had I lived with him for yet another sixteen I have no doubt that he would have remained just as much of an enigma.

Apart from her hours in the schoolroom and her social duties, few restrictions were placed on V S-W; her time was very much her own to do what she liked with. She describes herself in 1900 as

> always grubby and in tatters; my dogs, absorbingly adored; my rabbits, who used to "course" in secret with my dogs, and whose offspring I used to throw over the garden wall when they became too numerous; the trenches I dug in the garden during the war; the "army" I raised and commanded amongst the terrorised children of the neighbourhood; my khaki suit, and the tears of rage I shed because I was not allowed to have it made with trousers,— no, nor so much as a proper kilt; . . . [I] see myself, plain, lean, dark, unsociable, unattractive,—horribly unattractive! rough, and secret. Secrecy was my passion; I daresay that was why I hated companions.

It is clear that V S-W considered herself a disappointment to her mother, who openly reproached her with a lack of attractiveness and social grace, for nowhere has she ever recorded that her mother complimented her on her appearance or gave her any encouragement.

It is therefore interesting to see what references to her daughter Lady Sackville made in her diary. Personal comments are relatively few, considering that she was a regular and fairly voluminous diarist; up to 1904, when V S-W was twelve, most of the entries concerning her deal with colds and other childish complaints. There are, however, several references to V S-W's appearance, such as:

> The drawing of Vita's by Mr. Stock is finished and is quite pretty, but the child is much prettier and has far more depth and animation in her face. I took her to Mrs Freddy Bentinck's fancy-dress ball in her old fancy dress and powdered hair: she was lovely.

Lady Sackville's appreciation of her daughter's appearance was, however, apparently subjective: comments on her good looks may have been seen as a compliment to herself, and when she writes "Vita and I went to lunch at the Marlboroughs' at Blenheim. Vita was looking so pretty and was much admired," she quite possibly meant that she herself was flattered to have a daughter about whom people said nice things to her. Judging from V S-W's Autobiography, she does not seem to have passed the compliments on to her daughter.

V S-W must have felt that she was a disappointment to her father, too, although, unlike her mother, he never seems to have indicated in any way that this was so. She must have realized that he needed an heir to whom he could hand over Knole:

> Such a man, of course, ought to have had a smoothly running home; lots of children; sons whom he could teach to shoot and fish and ride and accept responsibility against the day when it should be theirs.

It is not surprising, in view of her mother's disparagement and her own sense of having failed her parents in some way, that V S-W suffered from a marked sense of inferiority which found expression in an attitude of defiance and pretended indifference to the opinions of others. This is clearly indicated in the following description she gave of herself:

> I think that between the ages of thirteen and nineteen I must have been quite dreadful. I was plain, priggish, studious, (oh, very!) totally uninspired, unmanageably and lankily tall, in fact the only good thing that could be said of me was that I wouldn't have anything to do with my kind. Seeing that I was unpopular, (small wonder, for a saturnine prig,) I wouldn't court popularity. I minded rather, and used to cry when I went to bed after coming home from a party, but I made myself defiant about it. I don't mean this to sound in the least pathetic; I wasn't unhappy, only solitary, but I don't pretend that I minded solitude, I rather chose it.

This defiance was also manifest in her attitude to school. Her early education had been at home, in the hands of a governess, but when she reached her teens, she was sent to Miss Woolf's school in London as a day-pupil. She makes no bones about her urge to compensate herself for her weaknesses:

> I set myself to triumph at that school, and I did triumph,—I beat everybody there, sooner or later, and at the end-of-term exams I thought I had done badly if I didn't carry off at least six out of eight first prizes. I think I was quite self-conscious over this: if I couldn't be popular, I would be clever.

Nevertheless, the nagging doubt has not been banished, for she continues with assumed bravado:

I wasn't hated at that school, at least I don't think so; I think they quite liked me. But I really cared not a scrap whether they liked me or not; those were my most savage years!

As V S-W grew older, the relationship between her parents deteriorated steadily. Their position was not always an easy one while old Lord Sackville was alive, for V S-W's father, although the heir, was not the son. After his death in 1908 it was rendered still more difficult by the lawsuit to decide the succession to the title, and, to an even greater degree, by the rather straitened financial circumstances in which they found themselves after paying death duties. This was not made easier to bear by Lady Sackville's utter lack of any sense of the value of money; quite capable of spending two thousand pounds on a diamond necklace on the spur of the moment, she was also capable of the most incredible economies the next moment. Thus she would buy note-paper from the most expensive stationer in London, but she seldom wrote her letters on anything but old scraps of paper that she did not like to throw away. One of her most satisfactory discoveries was that the toilet paper in the Ladies Cloakroom at Harrods made quite excellent notepaper, and she wrote on it to V S-W, *"Regarde, comme ce papier prend beaucoup mieux l'encre que le Bromo."*

The increasing strain between V S-W's parents led to ugly little scenes sometimes and brought out the ruthlessness in Lady Sackville of which V S-W was afraid. She writes:

I remember very vividly terrible scenes between her and Dada,— at least, she made the scene, he usually said nothing at all, or very mildly: "Oh, come, dear, is that quite accurate?"

And again:

There certainly *was* something ruthless about Mother, and one of the things that has left the strongest and cruellest impression upon me was a horrible little dialogue I overheard once in London, as I lay in bed in the dark next door; she was alone with Grandpapa, and was evidently very much annoyed over something, for I heard her telling him how much in the way he was, with that sort of *flick* in her voice that to this day makes me shudder; and he was moved to protest,—he, who never said a word! . . . I wish I could forget that little dialogue, but I can't; it burnt.

Up to the time of her marriage, V S-W must, in some respects, have been rather immature. Certainly as far as her mother was concerned, she seems to have been unable to adopt an independent outlook, and it was many years before she was able to look at her objectively and see her character as it really was.

In later life V S-W realized this herself, as she shows in her MS Autobiography, written in 1920, where she says that she had really only grasped that few of her mother's statements were accurate a comparatively short time before. The reason why she failed to realize this earlier, at an age when most young people have begun to understand the motives which drive their parents to act in the way they do, must have been that she was afraid of her mother's temper and was so completely dominated by her immensely strong personality. A clear indication of this can be seen in an entry in Lady Sackville's diary for 1910. The occasion was an amateur theatrical performance, in which V S-W had taken part, followed by a dinner-party at their home.

> I wanted to take Vita home, but she objected to come and got Lionel to support her and openly disobeyed me. I am extremely angry with L and V, with L for making V disobey my authority, as she ought to have changed at once and helped me preparing for the invasion that followed . . . Lionel came to speak to me and apologised for having interfered between Vita and me. Nothing could have been nicer than the gentle way in which he spoke—so I forgave him, but I stipulated very clearly that I wish to have full authority on Vita as I sh^d never make her do anything wrong against him. Vita came up to my room after dinner and sobbed till 12 o'cl, poor child.

V S-W was eighteen and a half years old at the time.

Although V S-W must subconsciously have hated her mother as well as loved her, she was no more proof against her overwhelming charm than any of the other people who met her. She was constantly being humiliated and trodden down, which, to a sensitive child, must have been agony, but at the same time she admired and adored her mother. She shows the ambivalence of her feelings when she writes:

> How my mother puzzled me, and how I loved her! She wounded and dazzled and fascinated and charmed me by turns. Sometimes she was downright unjust, and accused me of things I had never done, lies I had never told, . . . but how she could always win me

V. Sackville-West, 1910

round, however unjust she had been, just by looking at me and
saying: "Perhaps we have had a little misunderstanding." . . .
she had been really unjust, accusing me of telling a lie which I
happened not to have told; children are sensitive about such
things, and at the bottom of their hearts they know the difference
between truth and untruth; on this occasion I knew that I had
told the truth, but my mother made me kneel at her feet, which
humiliated me and hurt my pride, and said that I must ask God
to forgive me.

Lady Sackville always seems to have had this twofold power over
V S-W; at one moment making her suffer, either by humiliating her,
wounding her deepest feelings, crushing her or even by rendering
her acutely embarrassed; and at the next, inspiring in her a devotion
that was doubly strong for having been preceded by the diametrically
opposite emotion:

> Of course she always put me to acute embarrassment by the un-
> conventionality of her behaviour wherever she was; thus she
> always remained convinced that no one understood French ex-
> cept herself and me, and would make personal remarks at the top
> of her voice in that language. *"Mais regarde donc cette vieille horreur,
> ma chérie: qu'est ce qu'elle a l'air, avec cette perruque-là? Peut-on s'af-
> fubler ainsi!"* It was quite in vain that I tried to stem the flow of
> such comments whenever we went to a shop or to a matinée
> together . . . Oh yes, she was fun, she was enchanting, she was
> embarrassing, she made me feel hot with shame,—and then,
> seeing her visibly charm the tired shop-assistant behind the coun-
> ter, or watching her lovely profile beside me in the darkened
> theatre as she fanned herself with that unmistakably Spanish ges-
> ture, . . . I would have died for her, I would have murdered
> anyone that breathed a word against her, I would have suffered
> any injustice at her hands.

This ambivalence in V S-W's attitude to her mother must have
played an important part in the development of her character. For
many years she was haunted by her inability to come to terms with her
conflicting feelings about her mother, and this conflict is, as we shall
see, reflected in some of her writing during this time; in her books,
particularly the novels, the figure of Lady Sackville appears at times in
some guise or other, either good or bad. The two most obvious examples are Sebastian's mother, the duchess, in *The Edwardians* and the

domineering old Lady le Breton in *The Dark Island*. It was not until
after Lady Sackville's death in 1936 that V S-W seems to have been
able to write her out of her system with any degree of success. *Pepita,*
written in 1937, tells the story of V S-W's Spanish grandmother and
her family; in actual fact it would seem to be her own mother, Pepita's
daughter, that V S-W is analyzing and trying to explain to herself in
this book. After this date her mother figures very little in her works.

V S-W's CHILDHOOD WAS, in many respects, an unsatisfying, even an
unhappy one. An only child, much left alone with her old and queer
grandfather as her only true companion, lacking intimate contact
with the mother she adored and hated or with the father she loved
and admired, and suffering from a strong feeling of inferiority, she
was thrown back almost entirely on her own resources. She was singularly isolated and lacking in confidants. As she was educated at home
until she reached her teens, she had no school friends and, apart from
her grandfather, there was almost no one with whom she could as-
sociate on an equal footing. She was surrounded by servants, many of
whom she knew well and had had around her all her life, but, as she
says, "My child, remember who you *are*" was a phrase frequently to be
heard proceeding from the lips of governess or chaperone. She
played with the local children from Sevenoaks, but it is clear that she
did not play with them as equals; to them she must always have been
the lady from the great house, and she tyrannized over them, order-
ing them about with hereditary authority:

> I know I was cruel to other children, because I remember stuff-
> ing their nostrils with putty and beating a little boy with stinging
> nettles, and I lost nearly all my friends in that kind of way, until
> none of the local children would come to tea with me except
> those who had acted as my allies and lieutenants.

There were children's parties with her equals too; many of them,
for V S-W's diary contains numerous references to the parties she has
been to, but they were under the eyes of mothers, her own included,
and her feeling of inferiority would probably have prevented her
from being herself. She cannot have enjoyed these parties.

Then there were the frequent house-parties and entertainments
given by Lady Sackville at Knole. V S-W was expected to attend these,
but what she saw there was to inspire her with a revulsion for Society

that was to remain with her to the end of her life. This is apparent in several of her books, but it is most clearly expressed in *The Edwardians:*

> Leonard Antequil, watching them from outside, marvelled to see them so easily pleased. Here are a score of people, he thought, who by virtue of their position are accustomed to the intimate society of princes, politicians, financiers, wits, beauties, and other makers of history, yet are apparently content with desultory chatter and make-believe occupation throughout the long hours of an idle day. . . . He listened carefully, tabulating their topics. They were more interested, he observed, in facts than ideas. A large proportion of their conversation seemed to consist in asking one another what they had thought of such-and-such an entertainment, and whether they were going to such-and-such an other, . . . These parties of theirs, he thought, were like chain-smoking: each cigarette was lighted in the hope that it might be more satisfying than the last. Then investments bulked heavy in their talk, and other people's incomes, and the merits of various stocks and shares; . . . If this is Society, thought Antequil, God help us, for surely no fraud has ever equalled it. These are the people, or a sample of them, who ordain the London season, glorify Ascot, make or unmake the fortune of small Continental watering-places, inspire envy, emulation, and snobbishness—well, thought Antequil, with a shrug, they spend money, and that is the best that can be said for them.

The first chapter of *The Edwardians* seems, in fact, to be an accurate description of the life that V S-W must have led as a child. Sebastian and Viola, who may well represent the male and female aspects of V S-W's personality, suffer as she suffered from a mother's dominating character, feel the same lack of self-confidence, share the same love of Chevron/Knole.

Although V S-W's childhood can hardly have been a happy one, there was compensation, and there was escape—not physical escape, although she mentions quite casually that "I forgot to say that two or three times I tried to run away, but was always brought back." It was, perhaps, just because of her isolation that compensation and escape come to be of such importance to her.

The compensation was first and foremost Knole; the escape was writing.

The importance which Knole had both for V S-W's writing and

for the development of her personality can scarcely be overstated. From her earliest childhood she had wandered about the great house until she knew intimately every one of its three hundred and sixty-five rooms, its galleries, its fifty-two staircases, its seven courtyards. After being in the hands of the Sackville family for almost four hundred years, the whole house was filled with family history, and during her early life V S-W became imbued with a deep sense of family tradition. Several factors probably contributed to strengthen even further the bonds between her and Knole. Her isolation from people, her hatred of companions, "a trait I inherit from my family," her lack of true contact with her mother, her awareness of the rootless Spanish-gypsy strain in her; all these may have tended to make her seek identification with Knole as a symbol of permanence, as firm ground beneath her feet. She turned to Knole for companionship and endowed the house with a living personality:

> Knole is not haunted, but you require either an unimaginative nerve or else a complete certainty of the house's benevolence

Knole from the air.

before you can wander through the state-rooms after nightfall
with a candle, as I used to do when I was little. . . . But I was
never frightened at Knole. I loved it; and took it for granted
that Knole loved me.

IT WAS TO KNOLE that V S-W transferred the love that in other children is normally lavished on people. This feeling for Knole was so
powerful that places came to usurp the position of people in her scale
of values, as she herself admits when, many years later, she wrote in a
letter to Harold Nicolson:

> You know me well enough to know that people don't count very
> much with me. I love places (Sissinghurst, the Dordogne,
> Florence) far more than I care for people, and Rollo [her Alsa-
> tian dog] probably means more to me than any of my friends.
> And of course Knole . . . but that is a separate thing I can't speak
> about. That goes too deep.

This should not be taken to mean that she had no interest in people; she had. But she found personal relations with people so difficult
that she much preferred meeting strangers to her friends, and felt
more at home with her dog and in places which she found congenial
than in the company of people. As she once let slip in 1945 in a letter
to Harold Nicolson, "How much I prefer strangers to my friends."
The feeling of her inability to establish contact with other people
haunted her all her life. It is the theme of an undated poem that she
probably wrote about 1940:

> There are times when I cannot endure the sight of people.
> I know they are charming, intelligent, since everybody tells
>   me so,
> But I wish they would go away.
> I cannot establish contact with anybody;
> They are all unreal to me, the charming intelligent people,
> And I daresay I seem as unreal to them.
> Yet I am real to myself,—or am I not?
> Anyhow I delude myself into some sort of reality,
> But when they come, the charming intelligent people,
> I lose all illusion of reality, whether my own or theirs.

The depth of her feelings for Knole was probably unknown even
to herself until she finally had to abandon all hope of ever owning it.

As Knole was entailed, she must have grown up with the conscious knowledge that it could never be hers, that it must eventually pass to her uncle, Charles Sackville-West, and thence to his son, Edward, born in 1901. In 1903, when V S-W was not quite eleven years old, the idea seems already to be firmly planted in her mind, for Lady Sackville records in her diary:

> Took Vita with me to spend the day with Charles and be introduced to Eddie . . . and Vita was very nice to him in spite of her jealousy of him.

But however much one may understand the inevitable with one's mind, one is nevertheless quite unprepared for the strength of one's reactions when the event actually happens. In V S-W's case there was also the story of how Pepita's illegitimate daughter had become chatelaine at Knole to show her that the unexpected can happen. When, therefore, her father died in 1928 and Knole passed to her Uncle Charles, the blow was no less for being expected. Her love of Knole was so deep and so integral a part of her being that she never really recovered from the loss, and even in 1950, twenty-two years later, she could write to Harold Nicolson:

> Oh Hadji [her name for Harold Nicolson], my Knole, my Knole! I have just been writing to Uncle Charlie [Lord Sackville] to ask him if he could supply me with a key to the garden-gate. I always had a master-key, but it got lost during the sale at Long Barn. It isn't that I would ever want to use it; it is only that I would like to have it by me, in case on some summer evening I wanted to go there, as I have often been tempted to do, letting myself into the garden secretly, and I couldn't bear the idea of being locked out. Oh God, I do wish that Knole hadn't got such a hold on my heart! If only I had been Dada's son, instead of his daughter! I hoped that I had damped down the fire into embers, but the embers blow up into a flame at one breath, so easily.

Although she had the key of Knole, she could not bring herself to use it until 1961, one year before her death.

V S-W's awareness of her feelings about Knole must have been greatly sharpened by the lawsuit to decide the inheritance of the title in 1910, when she was eighteen years old, for upon the outcome of the case depended whether she would continue to live at the house or not. The relief and feeling of security engendered by the fact that her parents won the case would have made the ultimate loss of Knole an even greater tragedy for her, for who is proof against the conviction that a miracle may again happen? The fact remains that, when Knole passed to her uncle in 1928, something happened to V S-W that was to leave its mark on everything she wrote and thought.

ACCORDING TO V S-W HERSELF, she began to write in about 1904:

> When I was about twelve I started to write, (it was Cyrano de Bergerac that first initiated me to the possibilities of literature!) and I never stopped writing after that,—historical novels, pretentious, quite uninteresting, pedantic, and all written at unflagging speed: the day after one was finished another would be begun.

In fact, her memory seems to be at fault here, for her first novel, about Edward Sackville, is dated 1906, when she would have been thirteen or fourteen. She wrote it, as she did the following works, straight into a thick folio volume; they are remarkable for the almost complete absence of alteration and addition.

The following year saw the completion of two plays in French, "Le Masque de Fer" and "Jean-Baptiste Poquelin," and a novel in English, "The King's Secret." More important to her, perhaps, was the fact that she entered the *Onlooker* verse competition and won a prize. She comments:

> £1. I had won in the Onlooker verse competition. This is the first money I have got through working. I hope (as I am to restore the fortunes of the family) that it will not be the last.

It is rather touching to find out that the competition consisted of supplying the last line to a limerick, and that V S-W was one of five winners.

In later life V S-W was extremely secretive about what she was writing; her husband and children used to say that "we only really knew what she was thinking when we opened her latest novel." In those days, however, she used to show her books to her mother in manuscript. Lady Sackville writes:

> I have finished reading her book on Charles II, The King's Secret. It really is very good, if not a little too long in the dialogues. But the character of the boy Cranfield is well delineated. She

meant him to be her own self that she portrayed! And he is a dear, lovable child.

It is clear, however, that whatever she may have felt about her daughter's writing, Lady Sackville must have belittled its value to V S-W, discouraging her with faint praise and the cold voice of parental common sense. In *Chatterton,* the verse drama V S-W had privately printed in 1909, the following dialogue occurs when Chatterton, full of dreams about his future as a poet, comes home after winning a prize at school for the poem he has written:

> *Mistress Chatterton.*
>   These little follies and these little whims,
>   They mean so much to thee just now, dear son,
>   But in a few years' time thou wilt forget
>   That ever thou did'st love to sit and dream,
>   And that thy verse was as a god to thee.
> *Chatterton.*
>   So truly, mother, youth's ambitions fade
>   And pass away?
> *Mistress Chatterton.*
>   They do, and thou, poor child,
>   Wilt soon be smiling at the tragedies
>   That seem so serious and fill thy life.
> *Chatterton.*
>   And am I but a child?
> *Mistress Chatterton.*
>   At seventeen?
>   What else? A foolish child!

The main themes of *Chatterton* are two: first, the poet's uncertainty as to the value of his inspiration and writing. The stimulus he feels when his friend Archer reassures him of his genius and encourages him to break away from his home in order to devote himself to the great work he has to do. Then comes the reverse. The effect of Walpole's condemnation of Chatterton's writing as a worthless forgery is to make him so downcast and convinced of his failure as a poet that he destroys his own works before committing suicide. Chatterton, in the play, suffers from the same doubts, fears, and reactions to positive or adverse criticism as did V S-W herself. The second theme, the nature and origin of inspiration itself, was a subject about which V S-W felt less doubt:

Archer.
   And thou? know'st thou what inspiration means?
Chatterton.
   Do I? Who can tell? At any rate,
   I know what it may mean to leave the earth
   In spirit, while the body, dead machine,
   Unconsciously records the spirit's thoughts.
   My eyes, my hands, are strangers to me then,
   I scarcely know what they will make me do.
   I am not present, and my will is gone;
   Some other will compels me to obey,
   And sways me,—hell or heaven-born, who knows?

It is also significant that Chatterton considers himself and the importance of the work he is doing greatly misunderstood by his mother:

Chatterton.
   I love thee, mother, but thou pain'st me so!
   Thou dost not understand me; it is sad
   When those we love most, understand us least.

IN THESE EARLY YEARS V S-W spent some time away from Knole traveling in various parts of Europe. After Sir John Murray Scott had become a friend of the family in about 1900, it was the custom for them all to go to Paris and live in his apartment for some time every summer. In the autumn, the whole party would move up to Scotland for the shooting and fishing—Sir John was a keen sportsman despite his twenty-five stone. These summers in Paris meant a great deal to V S-W, who was acutely conscious of the grace and beauty of Sir John's apartment and Bagatelle.

From 1908 onwards V S-W, and sometimes her mother, took to spending springtime in Italy; the first year in Pisa and Milan, later in Florence, for which V S-W developed a great love. In the autumn of 1909, Sir John and Lady Sackville took V S-W with them on a tour of Russia, Poland, and Austria. Russia in particular made a deep impression on V S-W, who wrote on their return, "How much I loved Russia! those vast fields, that feudal life, that illimitable horizon,—oh how shall I ever be able to live in this restricted island?"

Nineteen hundred and ten was the year that V S-W "came out," a process that she found exceedingly disagreeable; fortunately for her, the death of King Edward VII saved her from a great many festivities.

However, at one small dinner party she met Harold Nicolson. She was eighteen; he was twenty-three, a young diplomat:

> The first remark I ever heard him make was "What fun!" when he was asked by his hostess to act as host. Everything was fun to his energy, vitality, and buoyancy. I liked his irrepressible brown curls, his laughing eyes, his charming smile, and his boyishness.

That summer V S-W was seriously ill with pneumonia. Lady Sackville rented a villa just outside Monte Carlo to which she took her daughter to spend the whole winter so that she should have every chance of recuperating quickly. Harold Nicolson (subsequently referred to as H.N.) was a frequent visitor when he was able to get away from Madrid, where he had been posted. After the usual spring visit to Italy, V S-W and her mother returned to Knole, where they spent the rest of the year.

In January 1912, Sir John died suddenly. A few days later H.N. proposed to V S-W. It was not, perhaps, the moment he would have chosen for the occasion, but he was to go to Constantinople at the end of the month and he wished to know where he stood before leaving. V S-W accepted him, but as Lady Sackville did not think H.N. an entirely satisfactory suitor for her daughter, who she considered would be marrying beneath her in accepting a man who would not be in a position to keep her as she was used to being kept, she refused to allow the engagement to be made public.

H.N. returned from Constantinople in August 1912. The moment was still not propitious for the announcement of their engagement, for Sir John's will was not yet proved, and it was known that his family were furious about the legacy to Lady Sackville and intended to contest it. However, H.N. and V S-W were able to spend the better part of two months together at Knole, after which they and Rosamund Grosvenor, a friend of hers, spent the following six months in Italy. When H.N. had to return to Constantinople in the spring, V S-W and Rosamund Grosvenor went on to Spain together.

The lawsuit about Sir John's will came to court in June 1913. When Lady Sackville had won her case, she gave V S-W and H.N. permission to announce their engagement and arrange the wedding for the autumn. On 1st October, 1913, they were married in the private chapel at Knole. V S-W writes:

> Mother, who doesn't like being émotionée, stayed in bed.

CHAPTER III

ꙮ 1913–1929 ꙮ

HAROLD NICOLSON WAS BORN IN TEHERAN IN 1886, the third son of Sir Arthur Nicolson (later Lord Carnock), a diplomat of Scottish family, and Catherine Rowan Hamilton, a younger sister of Lady Dufferin. His boyhood and youth were spent in the legations and embassies at which his father was stationed, in Constantinople, Sophia, Tangier, Madrid, and St. Petersburg, or at the Ulster houses of his mother's family. When he began school, he was sent first to a private school at Folkestone, and then on to Wellington College and Balliol. In 1909 he passed into the Foreign Office, having come second in the entrance examination, one of the most competitive of the day. The following year he met V S-W.

By temperament H.N. was entirely different from V S-W. He was gay, boyish, generous; the sort of man that people take an instant liking to. But at the same time he was an intellectual aristocrat, acutely conscious of the fact that he belonged to an élite of intelligence and achievement. He could be lacking in charity to those whom he felt to be his mental inferiors, and all his life he was prejudiced against most Americans, Jews, all colored and Levantine peoples, and most of the middle and working classes; failings of which he was aware. To those with whom he felt an affinity, however, he was a delightful companion, being by nature a good conversationalist and a person who loved good company.

The marriage between H.N. and V S-W was, despite the great differences in their characters and temperaments, an extremely successful one, although not without its perilous moments. It was, to use a hackneyed expression which here happens to suit perfectly, a true marriage of minds, for what, above all, attracted each of them was the intellectual quality of the other's mind.

V S-W regarded "Harold far more as a playfellow than in any other light. Our relationship was so fresh, so intellectual, so *un*physical, that I never thought of him in that aspect at all."

Even during their engagement this side of their relationship had been dominant in her mind:

> He was as gay and clever as ever, and I loved his brain and his youth, . . . I did like him better than anyone, as a companion and playfellow, and for his brain and his delicious disposition.

A few days after the wedding H.N. and V S-W left England to spend their honeymoon in Italy and Egypt before going on to Constantinople, where H.N. had to resume his duties at the Embassy. Six months later, with the threat of war growing ever closer, H.N. was recalled to England, where they arrived in June 1914. Shortly afterwards, their first son, Benedict, was born. V S-W writes:

> I remember a divine voyage by sea from Constantinople to Marseilles, through the Aegean, a second honeymoon. We met Mother in Paris, and both thought that she was going off her head, as she was obviously in an extraordinarily unbalanced state of mind. Then we went to Knole. War was declared on the 4th of August, and Ben was born on the 6th. Scenes immediately began with Mother over his name, and they culminated in our taking a house in London as it was impossible for us to remain with Mother. We spent the winter in London, and I became quite sociable.

The house they bought was 182 Ebury Street, in Pimlico—the house that Mozart had lived in when he was in London. It had belonged to Lady Sackville, who had had it largely rebuilt with the help of Sir Edwin Lutyens a few years before. However, even if V S-W felt that she could never again live at Knole for fear of further disagreements with her mother, it seemed that neither could she bear to be out of reach of it, for in the summer of 1915 she and H.N. bought Long Barn, a sixteenth-century house only two miles away from her beloved Knole. Here, in Kent, they used to spend every summer until 1925, when H.N. was posted to Teheran as Counsellor, when they

Long Barn.

sold the house in Ebury Street and moved to Long Barn permanently. In 1917 her second son, Nigel, was born in London.

These war-time years were probably the most contented of her life. She was able to see every day the husband she adored and there were only her children to distract her attention from him alone. Apart from the disagreements with her mother, she seems to have had no worries. She was writing poetry. When, in 1920, she looked back on these years, she said:

> That was the only period of my life when I achieved anything like popularity: I was no longer plain, I took adequate trouble to make myself agreeable, Harold was loved by everyone who met him, we were, in fact, a nice young couple to ask out to dinner. Oh God, the horror of it! I was so happy that I forgot even to suffer from Wanderlust.

IN 1917 V S-W ACHIEVED TRUE PUBLICATION when John Lane accepted her *Poems of West and East*. The themes of some of the poems in this volume are themes that are to recur time and again in her poetry, but here, in this first book, they are strangely muted and without the passion with which they are later to be stated. "To Knole, October 1, 1913" is a leave-taking of the house on the day of her marriage, but the note of anguish with which she was later to refer to Knole is not present. Only two of the poems, "Disillusion" and "Resolution," contain signs of the intensely personal self-examination and reflection which were to be characteristic of much of V S-W's poetry.

After the end of the war, H.N. was sent to Paris as one of the members of the British Delegation to the Paris Peace Conference. For the services he rendered there he was awarded the C.M.G. at the early age of thirty-four. However, his enforced absence from home and his family for considerable periods, the longest since their marriage five years before, helped to precipitate a crisis in his marriage.

As a child, V S-W had always been something of a tomboy, and fairly early in life she discovered that she was attracted to her own sex. It was in the summer of 1911, when she was nineteen years old, that her close friendship with Rosamund Grosvenor, whom she had known since she was six, gradually became something more, and in the following two or three years it developed into love. It was not, however, a love that ever touched her very deeply, for, as she was later to discover, the passionate side of her nature was never aroused. As she wrote herself, "my liaison with Rosamund was, in a sense, superficial. I mean that it was almost exclusively physical as, to be frank, she always bored me as a companion. I was fond of her, however; she was a sweet nature. But she was quite stupid." Nevertheless, V S-W was enough in love to wonder several times whether she would ever marry H.N.

Then followed the very happy years of her early married life with H.N., first in the Middle East, and then at Knole, London, and Long Barn. In April 1918, however, a chance meeting led to consequences which very nearly wrecked their marriage. V S-W had invited a friend who was bored to spend a fortnight at Long Barn. She was Violet Keppel, the daughter of Alice Keppel, who had formerly been King Edward VII's mistress. They had known each other since 1905, and even in those early days V S-W had felt a current of excitement and attraction in her company. Now, suddenly, this friendship developed into a passionate affair that swept them both off their feet, and within a month they were living together in Cornwall. In November they went to Paris, where V S-W dressed as a wounded officer and called herself Julian, and then on to the south of France, not returning to

Violet Keppel Trefusis, 1926.

V. Sackville-West, 1924.

England until March 1919. Violet Keppel, however, was half engaged to a man named Denys Trefusis, who was very much in love with her and was prepared to marry her on her own terms—that it should be a marriage in name only. By the time the two returned to England H.N., Lady Sackville, Alice Keppel, and Denys Trefusis all knew what was happening and pressure was being brought to bear on Violet to have her engagement announced, which it was shortly afterwards. The year that followed was a time which must have torn V S-W almost in two; physically she was passionately in love with Violet, and at the same time she was intellectually very much in love with H.N. Violet was doing everything in her power to get V S-W to leave her husband and go away with her, even after her marriage to Denys Trefusis on June 16th, 1919, and finally, on February 9th, 1920, V S-W crossed to France, to Amiens, where Violet was waiting for her, determined never to return. Five days later H.N. and Denys Trefusis flew over to try to persuade their wives to come back to them. At first, no argument was of any avail, but then H.N. asked V S-W, "Are you sure Violet is as faithful to you as she makes you believe? Because Denys has told your mother a different story." She immediately went down to the restaurant and charged Violet with having deceived her with Denys. When Violet did not give her a clear denial, she left her and returned to England with H.N. This was not the end of the affair, but the shock of believing herself betrayed gradually killed her passion for Violet, and by the end of 1921 she had more or less recovered from it, though not from the aftereffects. A bare statement of the facts, such as that given above, does little justice to the intense feelings and suffering of all those involved in this tragedy, and none to the great love and tact of H.N. in winning back his wife. Both are described with great tenderness and understanding by Nigel Nicolson in his book *Portrait of a Marriage*.

The aftereffects of the affair were several and lasting. The most immediate result seems to have been that when she returned to England she wrote an autobiography of her life as a child, her upbringing, and the whole story of the affairs with Rosamund Grosvenor and Violet Trefusis. She wrote it "urged by the necessity of truth telling" in order to clear her own mind about her situation, and added, "Having written it down, I shall be able to trust no one to read it." It is interesting to note, however, that she gave pseudonyms to all the people who figured in it. Although she wrote that she could trust nobody to read it, it seems quite likely that she had, nevertheless, the idea at the back of her mind that it might one day be published. It would have been quite consistent with her character. It is one of the contradictions of her nature, one aspect of the duality within her, that, beside the secretiveness which she herself stresses, there existed a confessional instinct, a need to absolve herself by writing, usually in some transmuted form, about the events which intimately affected her. It is connected with the honesty and frankness that formed such an important part of her makeup. The Autobiography is the supreme example of this instinct; a moving document written with great force, simplicity, and directness while the memory of the events which inspired it were still burning white-hot within her. Here she can say outright, veiled only under transparent pseudonyms, what she can convey only by symbol and allusion in the books she was publishing—in the nineteen-twenties people were not yet ready for this sort of tragedy, as the fate of Radclyffe Hall was to show. Secondly, it left its imprint on her writing, both directly and indirectly: directly in the novel *Challenge,* some poems in *Orchard and Vineyard,* and many of the poems in *King's Daughter* which, although not published until 1929, must have been written about this time, as the name indicates. There is a clear sexual undertone in a number of them, especially in the poem entitled "Goosey Goosey Gander." Indirectly, it influenced several of the books she wrote in the succeeding few years through the increased self-knowledge she had gained as a result of the affair. She was, perhaps for the first time, fully aware of the violence of her passions. Lastly, she was now confronted with the problem of her dual nature. Basically, this must have arisen out of her intense regret that she had not been born a boy, but it was probably complicated by her acute awareness of the gypsy blood in her. She was afraid of it; afraid it would appear in her as she thought it had in Lady Sackville, of whom she said, "it accounts for much of Mother, who at times is pure, undiluted peasant."

The conception of heredity played an important part in her early works, particularly those in prose; her first novel, published in 1919, was entitled simply *Heritage.* On the face of it, this is just a love story, but closer examination reveals that it is also something else. The background of the story is V S-W's own ancestry—Captain Pennistan from the Weald of Kent had met and fallen in love with a beautiful Spanish dancer, and had brought her home as his bride. But the story itself is not concerned directly with them. It is about the two granddaughters of the marriage, Nancy, whose appearance is purely English but

whose temperament is Spanish, her sister Ruth, whose appearance is
Spanish but who has inherited little of her grandmother's fire, and
about Rawdon Westmacott, her cousin, who has both her appearance
and her temperament.

To him Ruth is irresistibly drawn, despite the fact she hates him.

V S-W's conception of heredity in this book has been strongly
influenced by Francis Galton's experimental mating of a common
brown mouse with a dancing mouse. She mentions the experiment
and describes how "in the subsequent generations the common brown
house mouse predominated, but every now and then there came a
mouse that waltzed and waltzed, restless and tormented, until in the
endless pursuit of its tail it died, dazed, blinded, perplexed, by the re-
lentless fate that had it in its grip."

The central theme of the story is really the mutual attraction and
repulsion felt by Ruth and Rawdon—two facets of V S-W's character.
Ruth says, "He cringes to me, and then I bully him; or else he bullies
me, and then I cringe to him. But quarrel as we may, we always come
together again."

The narrator, who is also deeply involved emotionally, comments:

> Ruth loved me—she has told me so, and I know, without argu-
> ment, that she is speaking the truth—yet she found pleasure in
> the love of another man, and even a certain grim pleasure in his
> ill-treatment of her. Or should I reverse my order, finding more
> marvel in her humility under his caresses than under his blows?
>   What am I to believe? that she is cursed with a dual nature,
> the one coarse and unbridled, the other delicate, conventional,
> practical, motherly, refined? . . . And is it, can it be, the result of
> the separate, antagonistic strains in her blood, the southern and
> the northern legacy? Did she love Westmacott with the one, and
> me with the other?

These are surely the questions that V S-W feels have a personal
application for her, too.

Heredity and foreign blood were subjects that interested V S-W
very much indeed, and these themes occur in several of her books. On
one side of her ancestry was the Sackville blood, traceable back to the
Conquest, the blood that had already produced two poets. On the
other was Pepita's strain. She must have felt herself pulled in two di-
rections; wishing to believe in the strength of heredity for the sake of

the Sackville blood, and at the same time afraid to do so, because this would have meant that her gypsy blood was equally free to influence her. One moment she rejected the inheritance of her forefathers, the next she was compelled to admit it.

This conflict is clearly illustrated in an unpublished poem which she wrote in February 1928, an extract from which is quoted below. The thoughts contained in the poem were occasioned by her father's death.

Because I have your eyes
Does it mean I have your heart?
No, you are you, I am I,
Independent and apart.

Violently I refuse
All seisin with another,
Be she my kinswoman,
Be he my own blood-brother.

—Yet stay. Had he that lies
Dead in the chapel, not
The same unhappy eyes?
My father, that me begot?

This concern with her mixed blood and its possible effects on her personality is most noticeable in her early works. Nineteen hundred and thirty-seven is the last year in which foreign blood appears in her books. With *Pepita,* published the year after Lady Sackville's death, V S-W seems to have become reconciled with her origins, for the subject appears no more.

Duality, the Jekyll and Hyde personality, on the other hand, is frequently present in her works. In only one book, *Devil at Westease,* does this duality actually take the form of one person with two quite different personalities; Professor Warren—kind, gentle, and cultivated—and the great, but morally corrupt artist Wyldbore Ryan prove to be one and the same person, although the distance between their two personalities is so great that each speaks and thinks of the other as though he were a separate entity.

V S-W was perfectly aware of the duality of her own nature. In her short autobiography she quotes a comment made by Violet Trefusis:

The upper half of your face is so pure and grave,—almost child-like. And the lower half is so domineering, sensual, almost bru-tal,—it is the most absurd contrast, and extraordinarily symboli-cal of your Mr. Jekyll and Mr. Hyde personality.

H.N. shows his alarm about the same thing in a letter to V S-W:

What has always worried me is your dual personality. The one tender, wise and with such a sense of responsibility. And the other rather cruel and extravagant. The former has been what I have always clung to as the essential you, but the latter has always alarmed me and I have tried to dismiss it from my mind—or, rather, I have always accepted it as the inevitable counterpart of your remarkable personality.

V S-W must also have been alarmed by the more violent side of her personality. Eighteen months later she wrote what might be regarded as a reply to this letter, although it was actually occasioned by an exhortation from H.N. to give up the attitude that "it is silly to think that anything in life matters much":

Luckily for you, you have never seen the more tempestuous side of my nature. You have only seen an occasional bubble rising to the surface, which has startled you and made you realise vaguely that I feel passionately, and am vindictive and uncontrollable when my emotions are aroused, but as you do not like that sort of bubble, you have always wisely looked the other way.

The duality of V S-W's nature appears sometimes also to have influenced her in the choice between poetry and prose. Whereas her fiction frequently displays turbulence, strife, and even cruelty and vi-olence, her published poetry and nonfiction is often characterized by an underlying serenity of spirit, a quality noticeably lacking in the ma-jority of her novels. This is illustrated by the two books that she pub-lished in 1921, her second novel, *The Dragon in Shallow Waters,* and her second volume of verse, *Orchard and Vineyard.*

The novel is "a queer tale, . . . full of grimness and violence; a tale of two brothers, Gregory and Silas Dene, sinister figures, sprung of a sinister race, whose successive generations seem doomed to bear in some form or other, the marks of physical affliction and mental savagery. Of these brothers, Silas is blind, Gregory deaf and dumb, yet by sheer force of body and character they have established a kind of domination over their fellow villagers." Neither of the brothers is a whole man by himself—each needs the faculties only possessed by his brother in order to become one. They may be taken as representing two sides of a dual personality, an impression strengthened by the fact that they live in the opposite, mirror-image ends of the same double cottage. Gregory is basically a quiet and good man, and is creative—he designs machinery. Silas, on the other hand, is at bottom a violent man and produces nothing, the victim of a "ruthless savagery which always possessed him, without system or goal beyond a need to damage everything that was happy, prosperous, and entire." The conflict which arises because of this duality—Silas envies his brother his creative ability and peace of mind—drives Silas to the murder of his own wife, to inflict senseless suffering on animals, and finally to plan the destruction of Gregory and his wife.

If one turns from this harsh, tortured story, written at about the time when she was going through a personal crisis, to the volume of verse published the same year, one enters a different world. In *Orchard and Vineyard* there is none of the duality which is so obvious in the novel. Strong emotions are not absent—witness the poems entitled "Dissonance," "Bitterness," and "Insurrection"—but there is a homogeneity about the poems in that they are all spoken by what is recognizably the same voice, albeit in different tones.

One can trace a tendency to keep the two aspects of her personality in two separate compartments; the disharmonic fiction on one side and the more harmonic poetry and nonfiction on the other. It seems unlikely to be a mere coincidence. V S-W's attitude to what she wrote seems to indicate that she always placed a far higher value on her poetry than on her fiction. When, for example, in 1950, after a long period during which she had felt "really rather depressed by my inability to write the simplest thing," she had again started writing and was at work on a novel, the delight she felt was tempered by a regret that it was prose, not poetry, that had come back to her.

> Darling, I must write you another little note just to say how happy I am writing. It does make the whole difference in life. I just tell you this, because I like sharing things with you. I have been so miserable in the last two or three years not being able to write; really worried I have been, thinking that it was gone from me forever. I don't mean by this that I think my novel [*The Easter Party*] will be any good—you know that I am not a good novelist

—but at any rate it is exciting just doing it. It keeps me alive, living in an imaginary world which seems more real than the ordinary world. Of course I would rather write poetry. Perhaps that will also return to me one day.

Another indication of the probability that V S-W regarded her poetry as being more important than her other writing is contained in an article written by Jacques Vallette in the *Mercure de France* in 1949. His remarks have the appearance of being based on some personal communication between him and V S-W:

Elle a écrit en prose des biographies de saintes, l'histoire de sa grand-mère espagnole (*Pepita*), un roman (*The Edwardians*), de longues nouvelles (*All Passion Spent*). Mais elle s'estime soutout poète et veut être jugée sur une collection de vers écrits entre 1913 et la dernière guerre, auxquels s'est ajoutée en 1946 une autre séquence, *The Garden*.

V S-W's attitude to her novels is expressed very clearly in an interview she granted in October 1930, not long after *The Edwardians* had been published. When asked what she preferred writing, she replied:

Poetry every time. I only took to writing prose to fill up the gaps in between poetry writing. I now rather wish I never had! And I wish I could make a bonfire of all my novels . . . I don't like any of my books. Some I dislike more than others, but I can't say I like any of them. I particularly dislike my novels. The only one I can tolerate at all is *Seducers in Ecuador*. I prefer the poetry, books of travel and criticism.

As V S-W clearly valued her poetry higher than her prose, and as she was well aware of the darker side of her nature, it does not seem unreasonable to suppose that she gave freer rein to her conflicting emotions in her fiction in order to be in a calmer frame of mind to write the works to which she attached more importance. Her fiction writing might be described as a sort of catharsis.

IN 1920, H.N. LEFT PARIS, having completed his work at the Peace Conference. On his return he was appointed to a post at the Foreign Office in London, where he was to remain for the next four and a half years. During this time he and V S-W were living in Pimlico. In the summer, however, V S-W and the children moved down to Long Barn while H.N. continued to stay in London during the week, returning to Long Barn every weekend. One result of this arrangement was the continuation of the correspondence that flowed between them, a custom that had begun with their engagement in 1911 and was to continue until V S-W's death in 1962. Every day that they were apart each of them wrote to the other, and each kept all the other's letters. Each also kept a diary, but whereas H.N.'s was copious and informative, V S-W's contains little but a list of her engagements and a few quite ordinary comments. She was not the person to communicate her innermost thoughts to an ordinary diary except in rare instances.

IN 1922, V S-W PUBLISHED TWO WORKS. In May came *The Heir,* containing the long stort story which gives the book its title, and four short stories entitled: "The Christmas Party," "Patience," "Her Son," and "The Parrot."

"The Heir," with the subtitle "A Love Story," is the first expression of a theme that is to appear in other works by V S-W—the power of a house to affect a person's heart and outlook. The real hero of the story is not Mr. Peregrine Chase, the manager of a small insurance office in Wolverhampton, but Blackboys, the beautiful Elizabethan manor which has been left to him by the aunt he never met. He is persuaded to sell the house and estate in order to pay off the mortgages and have a small income left for his own use. Running through the story is a deep feeling of tradition, which the house and its contents symbolize. The influence of this, together with the sheer beauty of the house itself and its setting, work upon Chase until, almost despite himself, he is compelled to attend the auction and, at the eleventh hour, outbid the wealthy Brazilian whose bid would have given Chase financial security, though not Blackboys, for the rest of his life. Blackboys is Knole in a light disguise, and the story is dedicated to B.M., who is Lady Sackville (Bonne Mama).

The last short story in the volume, "The Parrot," has obvious personal applications. The bird in the story is kept in Pimlico, far from its native Uruguay, in a cage from which it is perpetually endeavoring to escape—indeed, it has twice succeeded in doing so. The motives given by the family for not releasing the bird are of the purest; they wish to protect it from cats, dogs, the English climate; but the bird will not understand. The poor little inefficient, downtrodden skivvy whose task it is to look after the parrot has transformed it into a symbol; her fifteen minutes with the bird each day are "the one fabulous excursion of her day; it was a journey to Bagdad, a peep into the caves of Aladdin. 'Casting down their golden crowns upon a glassy sea,' she murmured, in a hotch-potch of religion and romance." Then, one day, "the parrot no longer tore at its bars or screamed, and as for the under-housemaid, she was a transformed creature: punctual, orderly, competent, and unobtrusive. . . . It would have been hypercritical to complain that the girl's quietness was disconcerting." Soon afterwards, having left a note to say that she has gone to wear the golden crown, the girl is found dead on her bed, and the parrot dead in its cage.

The story is dedicated "To H.G.N."—V S-W's husband—and it must have been written some time about the end of 1921, very soon after the crisis in their married life. One can hardly doubt that the parrot represents V S-W herself, as does the skivvy, and that the transmuted symbol of the parrot is a glimpse of the splendor that reveals itself to the vision of a poet. How can H.N. have interpreted this story other than as a warning of what might be the consequences of any interference with her liberty?

It is not surprising that V S-W's first work of nonfiction should have been *Knole and the Sackvilles* (1922). Apart from the fact that it was a subject very close to her heart, she was also stimulated, and sometimes exasperated, by Charles J. Phillips, who spent the years from 1913 to 1922 doing the research for his own two-volume history of the house and family. She was stimulated by being able to watch a trained historian at work and following his progress; exasperated because he seemed so dilatory and vague that she wondered at times whether his book would ever be published. It was, eventually; in 1930. Without being in the least pedantic, V S-W's book is accurate and gives a long and interesting account of the house and its occupants through the centuries, enlivened by many small domestic details which make it an arresting study.

Although V S-W had probably not, in 1922, yet lost all hope of one day becoming mistress of Knole, she must have exercised considerable self-restraint to keep the tone of the book so light. Twenty-five years later, when Knole had passed into the keeping of the National Trust, she wrote a guide book to the house. On that occasion she wrote to H.N.:

I've done my proofs of the little guide-book I wrote for the National Trust on Knole. They bit. I am always fascinated, as you are, by the strange movements of the human heart. You see, I can write quite coldly and unmovedly a guide-book about Knole, and can also re-read it in proof, and then suddenly it will bite, like rodent teeth closing on one's wrist, and I wake to the truth, "This is *my* Knole, which I love more than anything in the world except Hadji [H.N.]," and then I can't bear to go on reading my own short little bare guide-book about my Knole, which has been given over to someone else, not us.

A few years earlier she had written a Diary Poem (unpublished) about Knole, aptly described by Nigel Nicolson as "like a lover to her," which further illustrates the strength of her feelings for a house that she regarded almost as a living personality.

Knole, when I went from you, you missed
One of your many children, specially?
God knows I gave you all my love, my agony,
Scarcely a stone of you I had not kissed.

Knole! Knole! I stretch my hands to you in prayer,
You, grey and solid; you, enduring, staid;
You do not know what surges beat against your walls;
Miss me a little, I who am your soul.

ONE OF THE IMPORTANT CONSEQUENCES of publishing *Knole and the Sackvilles* was that it led to the deepening of the acquaintanceship between V S-W and Virginia Woolf who, after reading the reviews, had written to the author. V S-W had sent her a copy of the book and had promised her a copy of her poems too, whereupon Virginia Woolf wrote:

I should never have dared to dun you if I had known the magnificence of the book. . . . . There is nothing I enjoy more than family histories, and I am falling upon Knole the first moment I get.
I am shameless enough to hope that the poems won't go to the wrong address.
I was prepared to sniff at Eddie's Georgians, and so I did: but not at yours.
I wonder if you would come and dine with us? Say Monday 8th, 7.45.

We don't dine so much as picnic, as the press has got into the larder and into the dining room, and we never dress.

This was the beginning of a long and intimate friendship between V S-W and Virginia Woolf which lasted until the latter's death in March 1941. It was to prove fruitful to them both.

In 1923 V S-W published three books. They were *The Diary of Lady Anne Clifford* and two novels: *Grey Wethers* and *Challenge*.

The first of these is an edited version of the diary of one of her ancestors. Daughter to the 3rd Earl of Cumberland, Lady Anne married in 1609 Richard, 3rd Earl of Dorset, the grandson of Thomas Sackville. A brief life of Lady Anne is included in *Knole and the Sackvilles,* but as this colorful and strong-willed woman had left a singularly detailed record of her long life, V S-W decided to edit it, publish it separately, and supply it with a long foreword.

Grey Wethers is an exceedingly interesting book. It is the story of Clare Warrener, the daughter of a scholarly squire, and her tragic love for Nicholas Lovel, a gypsy. Their tragedy "stands as instance and symbol of a more general theme—the conflict between powers of nature and those of culture and civilization." The setting, which is important to the story, is the heart of the Wiltshire Downs; a little village entirely surrounded by a prehistoric earthwork at the foot of what is, in actual fact, Silbury Hill. In the village stand the sarsen stones, the Grey Wethers.

There is a magical atmosphere about the whole story. The Downs themselves. Starvecrow, the house owned by Calladine, the man Clare eventually marries, the scenes enacted in the snow, are all surrounded by a supernatural aura:

> . . . an enchanted village built round the great monoliths called the Grey Wethers. . . . Everyone in King's Avon is under a spell; fantastic figures, unreal as a dream, mumble and mutter through the story. The lovers, Clare and Nicholas—he a simple village yokel, she a maid of high degree—the most unreal of all, move together, are separated, seek each other in the end and are united and mysteriously lost to the world that had known them. What became of them the reader is left to imagine "in the manner best suited to his own fancy and requirements."

The book also owes a debt to *Wuthering Heights,* which has clearly both provided the inspiration and influenced the development of the story. Clare, Lovel, and Calladine might well be regarded as V S-W's Catherine, Heathcliff, and Edgar Linton, and, as in *Wuthering Heights,* the landscape forms an integral part of the story; the Downs exert an influence on all who live in their shadow. V S-W has, however, adapted the story to suit her own needs. In Lovel and Clare (the name is symbolic: *claire*) she has introduced her own duality. "He was the darkness of the Downs, their threat, their solitude, their intractability; she was their light, their windiness, their sunlit flanks, their springiness of turf. United they formed a whole." This is stressed twice in the book. Symbolic of this duality, too, is Olver's mirror—one of the oldest symbols in the world of magic—in which, he says, each of them can see the image of the other.

In Calladine, V S-W seems, consciously or unconsciously, to have drawn upon and exaggerated all the negative characteristics which might be attributed to H.N. "He was a believer in dilettantism; but in the name of all good taste let it be dilettantism in graceful and becoming subjects." Furthermore, he "appeared satisfied, living with Clare a captive under his roof." The motif of the bird in the cage, which was so prominent in "The Parrot," is here repeated. Clare's thoughts constantly wander away from Calladine to the freedom of the Downs outside, and Calladine reproaches her:

> Always looking out Clare? what liberty do you see out there? you think I ought to let you go, little caged bird, but you would soon perish,—your pretty little limbs wouldn't stand the cold,—better stay happily where you are, believe me,—don't fret,—come back to me,—let me whisper how precious you are,—come back to our lovely idleness.

In *Grey Wethers* reappears the motif of the northern and the southern blood, first introduced in *Heritage,* this time in two physically separated characters, and again the southern blood is represented as being something to be regarded with suspicion, even shame. Lovel "had before him constantly the sight of his mother and brother to uphold him in the resolution that with the three of them the race must end. Such blood must not be carried on." This motif is also touched upon in *The Land,* here, too, with a feeling of revulsion:

> And then I came to a field where the springing grass
> Was dulled by the hanging cups of fritillaries,
> Sullen and foreign-looking, the snaky flower,

Scarfed in dull purple, like Egyptian girls
Camping among the furze, staining the waste
With foreign colour, sulky-dark and quaint,
Dangerous too, as a girl might sidle up,
An Egyptian girl, with an ancient snaring spell,
Throwing a net, soft round the limbs and heart,
                    . . .
A gipsy Judith, witch of a ragged tent,
And I shrank from the English field of fritillaries
Before it should be too late, before I forgot
The cherry white in the woods, and the curdled clouds,
And the lapwings crying free above the plough.

The third book V S-W published in 1923, *Challenge,* appeared
only in the United States, where it was praised for its wonderfully
described background, its story, and the fine writing. Although this
was the third novel she published, it was in reality the second that she
wrote; she began it on May 14th, 1918, and finished it in November
the following year, that is to say, in the middle of the affair with Violet
Trefusis. Julian and Eve in the story are very obviously V S-W and Violet, and the parents of both families insisted on the book being with-
drawn in England as they considered that the characters were far too
easily identifiable. The *New York Times* considered the novel "one of
the best that V. Sackville-West has written" and described it as

> a novel of the fine ardor and recklessness of youth. It is placed
> against a pseudo-historical background. The career of Julian Da-
> venant, the young Englishman, affords V. Sackville-West oppor-
> tunity for the fine mingling of two strains of action. First there is
> that colorful rendering of life on one of the Greek Islands, and,
> secondly, there is the more objective love affair of Julian and Eve,
> an affair that has its tragic implications but which is compact with
> the passion of youth. No possible notice of *Challenge* may be writ-
> ten without emphasis on the fine prose employed by the author,
> for there are times when it moves with an almost lyrical note. The
> subject matter is assuredly worthy of this method of narrative.

In 1924 appeared the first result of V S-W's growing intimacy
with Virginia Woolf. She had agreed that the Hogarth Press should
publish her next book, and on 7th June Virginia Woolf, who was
anxious to know when it would be ready, wrote to say that "it is very
good news that your story may be ready by July, or is it a poem?" By

Benedict Nicolson, Virginia
Woolf, V. Sackville-West, and
Nigel Nicolson, at Sissinghurst.

V. Sackville-West, 1924.

V. Sackville-West with Benedict and Nigel, at Long Barn, 1924.

the 15th September the manuscript was in Virginia Woolf's hands, and she had read it, for she wrote on that day to V S-W to let her have her reactions:

> It is not, of course, altogether thrust through; I think it could be tightened up, and aimed straighter, but there is nothing to spoil it in this. I like its texture—the sense of all the fine things you have dropped into it, so that it is full of beauty in itself when nothing is happening. Nevertheless such interesting things do happen, so suddenly—barely too. And I like its objectivity so that one can play about with it—interpret it different ways. . . . I am very glad we are going to publish it, and extremely proud and indeed touched, with my childlike dazzled affection for you, that you should dedicate it to me.

The book was *Seducers in Ecuador,* a short work of only seventy-four pages in a style that is reminiscent of that in the short stories of Henry James. In the opinion of the *Times Literary Supplement,* "What the tale fixes on as really devastating is the unlicensed spirit of imagination, which is never more hazardous than when it is conjured up by ordinary people."

The story is treated in a surrealistic manner throughout, the tone being set by Lomax's tinted spectacles, for "with a rapidity that he was never well able to understand, he found himself in such a position that he no longer dared to remove his spectacles at all; he could not face a return to the daylight mood; realism was no longer for him."

The first part of the story, from Lomax's marriage to Miss Whitaker up to his promise to Bellamy (note the names), takes place on the latter's yacht, aboard which there is a distinctly homosexual atmosphere. Much of the action takes place at sea, dissociated from place and, to some extent, from time, which imparts to the story a sense of universality. The last part, on the other hand, is enacted in the courtroom and in prison; a concrete reality which Lomax has to go through denuded of his tinted spectacles.

The story might well be described as an illustration of the inevitability with which Fate overtakes her victim, who, in this case, willingly submits to her decree. Miss Whitaker plays the part of the totally insignificant agent who is instrumental in bringing about disaster, in this case through her brother Robert, a shadowy, sinister Nemesis in whose existence Lomax does not believe, for "since Robert existed, what need had she to mention him?" His escape from this Nemesis is rendered impossible by his marriage to Miss Whitaker.

Added point is given to the whole by irony: the woman for whom Lomax has been waiting so long becomes free to marry him on the very day he weds Miss Whitaker; a post-mortem shows that Bellamy has never suffered from any fatal disease; Miss Whitaker is proved to be a virgin, and Lomax's motives are derided in court; the money Bellamy leaves Lomax, which is instrumental in directing suspicion to him in the first place, is never used for the humanitarian purposes for which Lomax has decreed that it shall be used. But "Lomax at night in his cell was almost happy: he was glad to endure this for Bellamy's sake. He had loved Bellamy." Lomax never resists his fate, is never surprised by the turn events take, and his execution is a sort of sacrificial death to which he willingly submits.

The book is unlike any other V S-W wrote, both in style and in tone. It is the only one of her books that a reader immediately recognizes as presenting difficulties in interpretation. The fact that, up to 1930 at any rate, V S-W herself liked it better than any of her other novels may be due to its very obscurity; she was, as she has stressed, a very secretive person.

IN 1925, H.N. WAS POSTED TO TEHERAN as Counsellor at the British Embassy. He obviously realized that after having had such a long spell in England at the Foreign Office he would have to spend several years abroad, for he sold the house in Pimlico and V S-W moved permanently down to Long Barn. Although separation was painful to them both, V S-W never considered accompanying H.N. on his tours abroad. To do so would have meant acting as hostess and becoming involved in the social life that she disliked so much. She did, however, pay two short visits to her husband in Teheran, in the spring of 1926 and again a year later. She has described her experiences in two books: *Passenger to Teheran* and *Twelve Days*.

On her first visit she traveled to Persia via Egypt and Basrah, whence she proceeded by rail to Bagdad and completed the journey in a car of the Trans-Desert Mail from the frontier of Irak over the mountains to Kermanshah, Kasvin, and Teheran. During her nearly two-month-long stay in the country she not only spent a considerable amount of time exploring the capital and its environs, but also made a journey to Isfahan by car.

In Persia she met a way of life that had remained unchanged for centuries, a society on which modern civilization had as yet made almost no impression and in which the craftsman still worked according to his ancient traditions. "But in the meantime the Europeans go on with their tea-parties, and their leaving of cards, and their speculations as to why some one was not to be seen, yesterday, at some one else's house." Her early life and the remembrance of the parties given by her mother at Knole had already left her with a distaste for what she considered the meaningless life of Society and, by contrast, an appreciation of the traditional and significant values which the craftsman and the laborer on the soil stood for. Her experiences in Persia undoubtedly gave renewed force to these prejudices and exerted an influence on *The Land,* which she was then writing, and on *The Edwardians,* published four years later.

Another effect of her stay in Persia was that it brought home to her once again the realization that places meant so much more to her than people. It caused her some concern, for she thought that:

> There must . . . be something a little wrong with some one who attached, instinctively, so much importance to place; . . . These brief but frequent fallings-in-love gave me cause for serious anxiety; such vibrations of response ought, I felt, to be reserved for one's contact with human beings, nor should nature have a greater power than human nature to excite and to stir the soul.

Her second visit to Persia, in 1927, strengthened her prejudices even more. On this occasion V S-W, H.N., and three other Europeans made a journey from Isfahan through the heart of the Bakhtiari Mountains to the Persian oilfields. Apart from the first and the last day's journey, the entire trip was made on foot and by mule. The story is recorded in *Twelve Days.*

Their arrival at the Anglo-Iranian Oil Company's sites produced a feeling of revulsion in V S-W:

> The contrast was so great as to produce an almost physical shock. . . . From constant contact with life reduced to its simplest elements, we walked straight into a hell of civilisation. . . . There were grocers' shops with the familiar tins and bottles on the counters; there were schools, and cool, organised hospitals; there were tennis-courts occupied by young women in summer dresses and young men in white flannels. There was, no doubt, society, intrigues, and gossip. One shuddered at the thought of it.

Another discovery she made on this journey, or perhaps first publicly revealed in the account of it, was that she was by nature one of those persons for whom solitude holds no terrors. On the contrary:

I write as one with a strong head for large draughts of solitude.
. . . To live encamped even within sight of the Bakhtiari Road,
that rude, violent, and occasional highway, would more than satisfy the misanthropy of most people. It would not satisfy mine.

V S-W probably started to write *The Land* about the middle of
1923. She had the admirable habit, when writing long poems, of dat-
ing each day's work, and the earliest passage of *The Land,* written
down in a one-hundred-page folio notebook obviously bought for the
purpose, is dated 5th June, 1923. The first draft of *The Land* shows
that, after this date, she added nothing more to the poem until 3rd
May, 1924, almost a year later. Even then, however, the poem progressed slowly; a little more was added in June and in November
1924, but then it was laid aside again until the following July. From
that time on, the poem progressed more rapidly, and each month saw
sections added to it until, on 8th December, 1925, the original version
of the poem was complete and was sent to the printers. The proofs
are dated 15th January, 1926. When V S-W left for Persia shortly afterwards she must have taken both her notebook and the proofs with
her; under the influence of what she experienced in Persia she made
quite a few alterations and a number of additions, some of them
lengthy, as the notebook and the proofs show. The last date in the notebook is 20th February, and the completed poem is dated Teheran,
April 1926.

There are two principal motifs in *The Land.* The first is a detailed
and loving record of the age-old ways of English agricultural life
made at a time when the old customs were rapidly dying out. As much
of what she recorded is in the oral tradition, it is clear that if she had
waited another twenty-five years or so before writing the poem, it
would hardly have been possible for her to write it in its existing form.

This had become apparent even by 1933, only seven years later,
for, in a review of V S-W's *Collected Poems,* which included *The Land,*
the *Times Literary Supplement* said that "the truth it tells has become
more urgently necessary; the world to which it invites our affections
and fancies, being more blatantly threatened, is already more precious."

Richard Church, in an article written on V S-W a few years later,
also stresses the great historic importance of the poem:

The Land is a picture of certain aspects of an England which is
vanishing; . . . Our social historians . . . have shown us the

seamy side of that bucolic scene; the gross brutality, injustice, covert slavery, squalor and filth. But in the bringing of those things to light, our historians have tended to neglect the positive qualities of a countryside held together by the pattern of the Feudal System and the rule-of-thumb Guilds. They have dismissed as superstition much of the lore of the peasant, and have failed to explain the secrets of his craft, secrets that were learned from no Trade Union handbook. They have neglected his personal delight and the simplicity of his relationship with the earth he tilled, the birds and animals he both loved and preyed on, the flowers he sometimes trod underfoot and sometimes set in the window of his mind, the God he worshipped in his village churches and objurgated in his week-day superstitions. It was left for the poets to record those things, and Miss Sackville-West has played a noble part in this preservation of something which is precious, and which is vanishing.

The second characteristic of the poem is V S-W's regard for tradition and the craftsman. Part of this feeling comes from her appreciation of the craftsman as a creative artist, for:

> All craftsmen share a knowledge. They have held
> Reality down fluttering to a bench;
> Cut wood to their own purposes; compelled
> The growth of pattern with the patient shuttle;
> Drained acres to a trench.
> Control is theirs. They have ignored the subtle
> Release of spirit from the jail of shape.
> They have been concerned with prison, not escape;
> Pinioned the fact, and let the rest go free,
> And out of need made inadvertent art.

Part of the feeling came from the pride she felt in her Sackville ancestry; the pride that was so necessary to her to counterbalance the presence of the gypsy blood she was so conscious of. Tradition was particularly important to this side of V S-W.

It was the reverse side of this intense feeling for tradition that made V S-W the unashamed conservative in outlook that she was,— the conservative who could write:

> *My Manifesto:* I hate democracy. I hate *la populace*. I wish education had never been introduced. I don't like tyranny, but I like an

intelligent oligarchy. I wish *la populace* had never been en-
couraged to emerge from its rightful place. I should like to see
them as well fed and well housed as T.T. cows, but no more artic-
ulate than that.

Although one of the reasons why she wrote *The Land* was the realization of the increasing threat of progress to traditional rural life, the
poem contains only indirect references to her dislike of modern
methods and bustle, such as when she refers to the thatcher, one of
the most highly skilled of craftsmen, as

> Brother to all the slow fastidious folk
> Whose care is matched by their disdain of time

or exhorts the harvester to

> Be prouder than the punctual rigid clerk,
> And stickle not to labour after dark,
> For you take nature's orders, he the clock's.

Direct criticism of modern life is not to be found until after her second trip to Persia when, after having lived a primitive life for a fortnight in the Bakhtiari Mountains, she experienced her return to civilization as a terrible shock. In *The Edwardians,* published in 1930,
occurs the scene when Sebastian, the young heir to Chevron, finds the
head carpenter with his eyes swimming in tears, and is told:

> It's my boy, your Grace—Frank, my eldest. Your Grace knows
> that I was to have taken him into the shops this year. Well, he
> won't come. He wants to go—I hardly know how to tell your
> Grace. He wants to go into the motor trade instead. Says it's the
> coming thing. Now your Grace knows . . . that my father and his
> father before him were in the shops, and I looked to my boy to
> take my place after I was gone. Same as your Grace's son, if I may
> make the comparison. I never thought to see a son of mine leave
> Chevron so long as he was fit to stay there. And Frank *is* fit—a
> neater-handed boy I seldom saw. That's what draws him to
> engines. Now what is engines, I ask your Grace? What's screwing
> up a nut beside handling a nice piece of wood? Such nice pieces
> of wood as I have lying out in the timber-yard, too; will be as ripe
> as a violin in forty years or so. Just right for Frank to handle by
> the time he's sixty. . . . I picked the oak for the grain myself . . .

"Frank," I said, "when you're sixty and need a nice piece of wood, you'll find it here, and don't you forget your father put it there for you." And now he wants to go into the motor trade . . . But it seems to me that everything is breaking up, now that my eldest wants to leave the shops and go into the motor trade.

AFTER HER RETURN from the second trip to Persia, V S-W wrote a short biographical work, *Aphra Behn: The Incomparable Astrea.* It is not altogether a successful venture, for some of the argument is contradictory and the conclusions are weak. It is interesting, however, for two reasons. Firstly, it is her first essay in this genre, apart from the long foreword she wrote to *The Diary of Lady Anne Clifford,* and secondly, it gives an insight into another of V S-W's own characteristics: her outlook on the rights of women.

She chose Aphra Behn as the subject of her first biography not so much because she was in possession of new information, although she had discovered three articles that she considered threw new light on Aphra Behn's early life; nor can it have been because she thought Aphra Behn a great, or even underestimated, writer, for she avows frankly "that Mrs. Behn, given her natural talent, prodigally wasted her opportunities." But "the fact that she wrote is more important than the quality of what she wrote. The importance of Aphra Behn is that she was the first woman in England to earn her living by her pen."

Though certainly not a feminist in the accepted sense of the word, V S-W had strong feelings about a woman's right to an independent existence. Dr. Bernbaum had made allegations about Aphra Behn which, if true, would have deprived her of a good deal of her glory, and V S-W seems to have been stung by these into defending her.

As far as V S-W herself was concerned, this feeling about a woman's rights took the form of a violent dislike of anything that tended to rob her of her personal identity. For example, she was always very annoyed if she were ever referred to as an authoress or a poetess. H.N. records:

> In the evening we listen to a broadcast by Vita on the Home Service. She is furious because they introduce her as "V. Sackville-West, the well-known authoress." She had managed to persuade them not to call her "Lady Nicolson" or "Miss Sackville-West" or

"Miss Victoria Sackville-West," but had omitted to warn them not to put "author" in the feminine.

Above all, however, it was the fact that as a married woman she was officially known by her husband's name that infuriated her. When she had to fill in a passport application form in the name of Mrs. Harold Nicolson she wrote:

> This, as always, has flung me into a rage. You know I love you more than anybody has ever loved anybody else, but I really do resent being treated as if I were your dog. The whole thing is an insult to human dignity, and ought to be revised. One is allowed no separate existence at all, but merely as a dependent upon whomever one marries. Why not get me a collar with your name and address engraved upon it?

The reason why she felt so strongly about her name is undoubtedly largely connected with her feelings for Knole and her ancestry, as the following extract from an unpublished poem will show:

> I will hold to my own, old name,
> Walled within walls of Knole;
> I will not sink my pride, my soul,
> In another's pride and fame.

Another illustration of the importance to her of her name is the following extract from H.N.'s diary about an appeal she made for the National Trust:

> I go . . . to the recording room . . . just in time to hear Vita announced as Miss Victoria S-W. I expect a row, but she does her piece with swan-like calm. Only at the end, when she has to give her name and address, does she fling into the initial "V" all the loathing which she has of her full name, or of my name, or of any name except V. S-W.

Her extension of this dislike to include being referred to as an authoress or poetess is merely the logical consequence of this.

IN 1928 VIRGINIA WOOLF published *Orlando*. She had begun to think of writing some book on an entirely new pattern as early as June 1925,

V. Sackville-West, *c.* 1927.

"Orlando on her return to England."

perhaps as a result of Lytton Strachey's suggestion that she should try "something wilder and more fantastic [than *Mrs. Dalloway*], a framework that admits of anything, like *Tristram Shandy*," but had done little more than think about it until October 1927. By 22nd October that year, however, she was able to note in her diary: "I am writing *Orlando* half in a mock style very clear and plain, so that people will understand every word. But the balance between truth and fantasy must be careful. It is based on Vita, Violet Trefusis, Lord Lascelles, Knole, etc." The "very clear and plain" is an irony, of course, but with the help of V S-W's MS Autobiography, which Virginia Woolf must have read before she wrote *Orlando*, it is easy enough to identify Violet Trefusis as the Princess Marousha Stanilovska Dagmar Natasha Iliana Romanovitch (usually known as Princess Sasha) and the sailor with whom Orlando finds her on one occasion as Mr. Trefusis, to take two examples only.

Until very recently, this brilliant book, which is so very different from anything else Virginia Woolf wrote, received far less attention than it deserves. This is almost certainly due to the difficulty of deciding to what category the book belongs. It has the subtitle "A Biography," which indeed it is, but it is presented in so esoteric a manner that few critics have chosen to give more than a cursory account of it. Now that Nigel Nicolson and Joanne Trautmann have published their books, both of which deal with *Orlando*, we may, however, expect a critical work which does justice to this highly original book, gives it its rightful place among Virginia Woolf's other works, and shows how she has enriched the art of biography by the way in which she has developed the ideas of Lawrence Sterne.

Orlando throws an interesting light on the marriage between V S-W (Orlando) and H.N. (Marmaduke Bonthrop Shelmerdine Esq.) as seen through the eyes of Virginia Woolf. As Herbert Marder says:

> Orlando and her husband Shelmardine [sic], on the other hand, are truly androgynous, the two sexes within them almost evenly balanced. It is because of the fineness of the balance that Orlando must constantly be shifting back and forth, that is, conforming her outer sex to changes in the inner weather. For the dramatic change of sex is only the first of many changes that follow without fanfare. The state of things becomes apparent shortly after Orlando's transformation into a woman.

Marder then goes on to quote the words of the narrator of the story, who finds that "she [Orlando] was censuring both sexes equally, as if

Harold Nicolson.

she belonged to neither; and indeed, for the time being, she seemed to vacillate; she was man; she was woman; she knew the secrets, shared the weaknesses of each. It was a most bewildering and whirligig state of mind to be in."

In James Hafley's interpretation of Virginia Woolf as a novelist there is an interesting comment on the fact that Orlando and Shelmerdine are from the first moment in such perfect communion with each other:

> The mentally androgynous man and woman can understand each other with a perfection impossible to those barred behind the limitations of their sex. When Orlando and Marmaduke meet, they understand each other immediately: "An awful suspicion rushed into both their minds simultaneously:
> 'You're a woman, Shel!' she cried.
> 'You're a man, Orlando!' he cried."
> The truth is that both are androgynous.

James Hafley's perceptiveness is quite correct. As Virginia Woolf well knew, both V S-W and H.N. were homosexual. Each was perfectly aware of the other's affairs, and neither made any attempt to conceal them from each other or from close friends. Their wonderfully successful marriage was, it must be repeated, based on intellectual, not on physical, attraction.

ANDREW MARVELL WAS A POET who interested V S-W, partly because he "was open to *direct* inspiration. . . . The source of his direct inspiration was nature; orderly, detailed nature; nature as he saw it in England." This interest was heightened because, although he lived in an age in which "flashes of personal intimacy and the desire for identification with nature were common to English poets in Marvell's age, as in nearly every other," there was nevertheless a difference between him and his contemporaries:

> To Marvell, in the brief years of his poetic creation, the mood was constant. . . . Conceits, when they occurred, were an ornament—or shall I say a disfigurement?—rather than an integral part; his real mood, in these nature poems, was the mood of seeing, and feeling; the mysticism which arose as their accompaniment was no conceit, but an inevitable consequence, familiar to

everyone who has ever entered into a moment of communion
with nature; and, as such, expressed by him in a manner readily
distinguishable from the cerebral exertions of his colleagues.

Here V S-W stresses the significance of the spirit of an age. After
saying that "it was not to be expected that Marvell should go free of
conceits and 'wit,' or that he should resist the temptations of screwing
his mind round into the prevailing contortions in the pursuit of some
over-complicated and over-subtle conception of the universe or of his
own consciousness," she explains her meaning by adding: "So strong,
so instinctive, is the habit of mind of one's own age, that the conceits
of the metaphysical poets—to us frequently so tortured and so extravagant—to them formed an intrinsic part of the process of poetic expression."

It is now possible to see more fully why Marvell should have such
a strong attraction for V S-W. She, too, was open to direct inspiration
from nature as she saw it in England, as she considered Marvell had
been, and, like him, she was a poet not altogether in harmony with the
habit of mind of her own age:

> What worries me a bit is being so out of touch with poetry as it is
> being written today. I see that the influence of Tom Eliot and the
> Spender-Auden school is paramount, yet I cannot get into gear
> with it at all. It is just something left out of my make-up.

IN 1927, H.N. WAS TRANSFERRED from Teheran to Berlin. Once
again V S-W refused to accompany him; she remained at Long Barn,
writing. H.N. was making a success of his career as a diplomat. At
Berlin he was the second-ranking official at an important Embassy
where, for a time, he acted as Chargé d'Affaires. If he continued in
the Service he could be sure of getting an Embassy sooner or later. On
the other hand, much as he loved his work, he realized that it would
inevitably entail a future with many years of enforced separation
from V S-W.

In 1921 H.N. had started to write books. By 1927 he had published one novel, four works of literary biography, one of general biography, and one on the development of English biography. Moreover, friends in England, notably Leonard and Virginia Woolf, had
told him that he was wasting his talents in diplomacy; he should be a
writer or enter politics. There were, however, certain impediments

against taking either of these courses. One of them was that Lady Sackville had been paying V S-W the sum of £1,600 a year under a trust settlement made when they were married. With increasing age, however, Lady Sackville was becoming more and more eccentric, at times being quite capable of accusing the Nicolsons of stealing her furniture, her jewels or her money, or of refusing to allow her to place a wreath on Lord Sackville's grave. H.N. and V S-W therefore wished to renounce this settlement, but as a civil servant his salary would not have been large enough for them to do so; nor could authorship alone guarantee him an income large enough to make them independent of Lady Sackville were he to leave the diplomatic service. For the time being the only possible course was to continue as they were.

From time to time H.N. came home on leave, but at the end of each period came the anguish of parting. This anguish was greatest for V S-W. It is probably true of her to say that she could give H.N. only one side of her love, but for her that was the vitally important one—the light side of her nature—and she gave it to him completely and without stint. With the passing of the years her love for him grew stronger, and each parting more painful. On 25th June, 1929, she was moved to write in a long letter after coming home from seeing him off at the station:

> What is so torturing when I leave you at these London stations and drive off, is the knowledge that you are *still there*—that, for half an hour or three-quarters of an hour, I could still return and find you . . .
>
> I came straight home, feeling horribly desolate and sad, driving down that familiar and dreary road. I remembered Rasht and our parting there; our parting at Victoria when you left for Persia; till our life seemed made up of partings, and I wondered how long it would continue . . .
>
> Then I came home, and it was no consolation at all. You see, when I am unhappy for other reasons, the cottage is a real solace to me; but when it is on account of *you* that I am unhappy (because you have gone away), it is an additional pang—it is the same place, but a sort of mockery and emptiness hangs about it—I almost wish that just *once* you could lose me and then come straight back to the cottage and find it still full of me but empty of me, then you would know what I go through after you have gone away . . .

You are dearer to me than anybody ever has been or ever could be. If you died suddenly, I should kill myself as soon as I had made provision for the boys. I really mean this. I could not live if I lost you. I do not think one could conceive of a love more exclusive, more tender, or more pure than I have for you. I think it is immortal, a thing which happens seldom.

Darling, there are not many people who would write such a letter after sixteen years of marriage, yet who would be saying therein only one-fiftieth of what they were feeling as they wrote it. I sometimes try to tell you the truth, and then I find that I have no words at my command which could possibly convey it to you.

When, a month later, H.N. was told that Lord Beaverbrook, who was looking for a suitable man to edit a page like the Londoner's Diary in the *Evening Standard,* had said that he would be interested in retaining him at a salary of £3,000 a year which could be supplemented by outside literary work, H.N. felt that the matter should be given serious consideration.

It was a difficult decision to make. Against the certainty of success in the Diplomatic Corps, which he loved, he had to place the uncertainty of the newspaper world and his doubts as to whether he would feel at home with the sort of writing he would be expected to do there, but also the chance of being able to live in England and free himself from the necessity of accepting Lady Sackville's endowment. In September he decided to accept Beaverbrook's offer and handed in his resignation to the Foreign Office. On 20th December, 1929, he left Berlin and on 1st January the following year he began work at the *Evening Standard.*

CHAPTER IV

⚘ 1930–1946 ⚘

WHEN H.N. JOINED THE STAFF of the *Evening Standard* on 1st January, 1930, a great change took place in the Nicolsons' lives. In the first place, in order to be near his office, H.N. took chambers in London in February; No. 4, King's Bench Walk, in the Inner Temple. There he and V S-W lived during the week for the next few months, returning to Long Barn at the weekends. This they were able to do as both their sons were at boarding school by this time; Benedict, aged 15, was at Eton, and Nigel, aged 12, at Summer Fields, Oxford.

In the middle of March that year a disturbing rumor reached them that the property next to Long Barn was to be sold to a large poultry firm. Faced with this threat to their neighboring fields, the Nicolsons first tried to buy the land themselves, but as the price was high, they decided to look around the Weald of Kent and Sussex for another house where they could live unmolested. On 4th April "Vita telephones to say she has seen the ideal house—a place in Kent near Cranbrook, a sixteenth century castle," and the following day the whole family went to have a look at it. When they revisited the castle the following day they decided to consider buying it.

Sissinghurst Castle had once been a great Tudor mansion, the home of Sir John Baker in the reign of Henry VIII. It was his daughter, Cicely, who had married Thomas Sackville in 1554. The castle had deteriorated since the middle of the eighteenth century, when Horace Walpole had described it as "a house in ruins and a park in ten times greater ruins." Four years after his visit, it was leased to the Government as a prison for French sailors captured in the Seven

Sissinghurst Castle, the library and tower, built in the fifteenth and sixteenth centuries.

Years War. Sissinghurst had never recovered from that experience; a large part of it had been pulled down about 1800, and for nearly sixty years after that, the remaining buildings had been used as the parish work-house. Since 1845 it had been a romantic, if neglected, adjunct to a farm. Some of the surviving buildings had been used as stables and outhouses, others as dwellings for farm laborers. When H.N. and V S-W looked at it, there was not a single room that they could immediately occupy and the garden was a vast rubbish heap.

It was a depressing sight, and a great deal of imagination must have been needed to see what could be made of it. H.N.'s mother, Lady Carnock, was very much against the idea when she saw it a few days later, which caused H.N. and V S-W to hesitate for some time before deciding to buy it. But on 24th April H.N. wrote V S-W a letter which finally settled the matter in their minds.

My view is:
(a) That it is most unwise of us to get Sissinghurst. It costs us £12,000 to buy and will cost another good £15,000 to put it in order. This will mean nearly £30,000 before we have done with it. For £30,000 we could buy a beautiful place replete with park,

garage, h. and c., central heating, historical associations, and two lodges r. and l.

(b) That it is most wise of us to buy Sissinghurst. Through its veins pulses the blood of the Sackville dynasty. True it is that it comes through the female line—but then we are both feminist and, after all, Knole came in the same way. It is, for you, an ancestral mansion: that makes up for the company's water and h. and c.

(c) It is in Kent. It is in a part of Kent we like. It is self-contained. I could make a lake. The boys could ride.

(d) We like it.

A fortnight later, on 7th May, they bought it.

Of the two, it was certainly V S-W who was the driving force behind making the decision to buy the castle. She had wanted Sissinghurst from the first moment she saw it, partly, no doubt, because she saw what could be done with it, ruin though it was, but the main reason was almost certainly another. Two years before this, she had finally lost any hope she may have had of keeping Knole. Her father had died in February 1928, and her uncle, Charles Sackville-West, had succeeded to both Knole and the title. She must have felt that it was no longer her home and did not, in fact, visit Knole again until 1961, shortly before her death. H.N. pinpointed the real reason for her eagerness to buy Sissinghurst when he wrote "Through its veins pulses the blood of the Sackville dynasty. . . . It is, for you, an ancestral mansion."

Having bought Sissinghurst, H.N. and V S-W threw themselves with great energy into the task of putting the grounds and the buildings to rights. There was an immense amount to be done just to make the existing buildings habitable, for they were all in a state of considerable dilapidation; it was not until October 1930 that they were able to sleep there. But H.N. and V S-W also planned to transform the grounds into something that was to become one of the show gardens of England. A start on this project was made early in 1931, but it was not until the end of 1937 that the bulk of the work was finished.

After the rootless years which followed her marriage to H.N. and the subsequent departure from Knole, years during which she had not been living at any place to which she could feel that she had any permanent attachment, the purchase of Sissinghurst must have been very important to V S-W. It was not only that the castle gave her a link with the past, a sort of replacement for Knole; the work of creating a

Harold Nicolson and V. Sackville-West, *c.* 1936, at Sissinghurst.

garden gave her a purpose in life, apart from her writing, which could keep her fully occupied at a time of life which might otherwise have proved difficult for her. Leonard Woolf has summed up well how much the garden at Sissinghurst meant to V S-W:

> As the thousands of people who every year visit Sissinghurst know, she restored a good deal of the castle and created a garden of very great beauty.
>
> In the creation of Sissinghurst and its garden she was, I think, one of the happiest people I have ever known, for she loved them and they gave her complete satisfaction in the long years between middle age and death in which for so many people when they look out of the windows there is only darkness and desire fails.

V S-W described her own feelings in the short poem "Sissinghurst," written in 1930. A "tired swimmer in the waves of time," she has found

> . . . the castle and the rose.
> Buried in time and sleep,
> So drowsy, overgrown,
> That here the moss is green upon the stone,
> And lichen stains the keep.

She was able to identify herself with the castle in a way that she had never been able to do with other places at which she had lived since her marriage because of its connection with the Sackvilles, "by birthright, far from present fashion."

In these surroundings she could escape from the modern world and "sink down through centuries to another clime," to a sanctuary which seemed

> . . . an image, water-drowned,
> Where stirs no wind and penetrates no sound,
> Illusive, fragile to a touch, remote,
> Foundered within the well of years as deep
> As in the waters of a stagnant moat.
> . . .
> As no disturber of the mirrored trance
> I move, and to the world above the waters
> Wave my incognisance.

In the security given her by the castle, and surrounded by the age-old methods of agriculture which meant so much to her, she feels capable of recovering from the loss of Knole and creating something anew:

> Beauty, and use, and beauty once again
> Link up my scattered heart, and shape a scheme
> Commensurate with a frustrated dream.

Although V S-W never recovered completely from the loss of Knole, she developed an almost equally strong and very possessive love of Sissinghurst. In 1958, she cut H.N. out of the running of the castle, which was to be entirely hers, and her reactions when she heard that Nigel Nicolson had discussed the possibility of one day handing Sissinghurst over to the National Trust were almost hysterical:

> H. said that Nigel had sounded him on whether I would ever consider giving Sissinghurst to the National Trust. I said, Never, never, never! *Au grand jamais, jamais.* Never, never, never! Not that hard little metal plate at my door! Nigel can do what he likes when I am dead, but so long as I live, no National Trust or any other foreign body shall have my darling. No, no. Over my corpse or my ashes, not otherwise. No, no. I felt myself flush with rage. It is bad enough to have lost my Knole, but they shan't take Sissinghurst from me. That at least is my own. *Il y a des choses qu'on peut pas supporter.* They shan't; they shan't; I won't. They can't make me. I *won't.* They can't make me. I never would.

In spite of the fact that the restoration of the castle and the creation of a great garden occupied a considerable amount of her time, she does not appear to have devoted less time to her writing than she did before, for during the years in which she was at work on the garden she published four full-length novels, her collected poems, and *Pepita.* In fact, as she wrote to H.N. one rainy day, she felt "how fortunate we both are to have both indoor and outdoor occupations. If we can't garden, we can write."

In May 1930, V S-W published the first of these books, *The Edwardians.* This was, as Leonard Woolf remarked,

> a novel about Knole, the Sackvilles, and Edwardian Society with the most aristocratic capital S, written from the inside of not only

Knole, but also Vita. Inside Vita was an honest, simple, sentimental, romantic, naïve, and competent writer. When she let all this go off altogether in a novel about high life, she produced in *The Edwardians* a kind of period piece and a real best-seller. . . . We sold nearly 30,000 copies of *The Edwardians* in the first six months, and by the end of the year the Press had made a profit of nearly £2,000 on it. It has gone on selling for years.

Leonard Woolf's summary of the contents of the book is correct as far as it goes, but is far from adequate. For one thing, as S. P. B. Mais pointed out, "Quite apart from its interest as a human story, it is an historical document of great importance." It describes the Edwardians themselves, the very highest society, chiefly the fast set but also the intensely respectable set which was gradually even then decaying, though its power was still immense.

It is not, however, a one-sided picture that V S-W presents. Her strong feeling for tradition and the consciousness of her aristocratic background on one hand and, on the other, the dislike she had felt for what she had regarded as the artificiality and uselessness of the society life her mother had indulged in, are here in conflict.

Sebastian states one side of the problem when he discusses the future of Chevron—Knole—and himself with his sister Viola:

I will agree with you that Chevron, and myself, and Wickenden, and the whole apparatus are nothing but a waxwork show, if you like. Present-day conditions have made us all rather meaningless. But I still think that that is a pity. I think we had evolved a good system on the whole, which made for a good understanding between class and class. Nothing will ever persuade me that the relations between the squire and the craftsman, or the squire and the labourer, or the squire and the farmer, don't contain the elements of decency and honesty and mutual respect. I wish only that civilisation could have developed along these lines.

The reverse side of the medal, the empty selfishness of the fast set, relieved only by their rigid adherence to a code of behavior, has been mentioned previously. Numerous instances are to be found in the book, such as when Viola enlightens a rather naïve young girl of her acquaintance as to the true nature of society:

Very well, if you want the truth, here it is. The society you live in is composed of people who are both dissolute and prudent. They want to have their fun, and they want to keep their position. They glitter on the surface, but underneath the surface they are stupid—too stupid to recognise their own motives. They know only a limited number of things about themselves: that they need plenty of money, and that they must be seen in the right places, associated with the right people. In spite of their efforts to turn themselves into painted images, they remain human somewhere, and must indulge in love-affairs, which sometimes are artificial, and sometimes inconveniently real. Whatever happens, this world must be served first. In spite of their brilliance, this creed necessarily makes them paltry and mean. Then they are envious, spiteful, and mercenary; arrogant and cold. As for us, their children, they leave us in complete ignorance of life, passing on to us only the ideas they think we should hold, and treat us with the utmost ruthlessness if we fail to conform.

V S-W's concern with the good and evil sides of an oligarchical society seems quite understandable in view of her childhood experiences and her natural outlook. What perhaps strikes one as a little more surprising is the basically socialist solution which is here and there put forward, both in *The Edwardians,* and in *Family History,* which deals to a great extent with the same question. It might not seem to be in keeping with the general tenor of V S-W's ideas. The explanation is quite possibly to be sought in the influence of Virginia and Leonard Woolf. The characters of Viola and Leonard Antequil, who figure in both these books, particularly in *Family History,* clearly owe a great deal to the Woolfs, who have obviously inspired them, and in both books it is Viola and Leonard, especially the former, who put forward the radical suggestions.

Finally, *The Edwardians* is partly biographical. The first two chapters in particular, describing Sebastian's childhood and the organization and running of a great country house, give a detailed and probably highly accurate description of life at Knole as V S-W knew it in the first decade of this century.

"We published *The Edwardians* in 1930" writes Leonard Woolf, "and *All Passion Spent,* which she wrote in less than a year, in 1931. This was, I think, the best novel which she ever wrote, though there was rather more than a touch of sentimentality in it. It did very well, though not as well as *The Edwardians,* selling about 15,000 copies in the first year—it still sells 35 years after it was first published—and showing a profit of about £1,200."

The subject of the novel has been variously described as "a study of extreme old age . . . the unusual feat is actually accomplished here of presenting old age as something worth creating in itself . . . and that period of life which new young writers have delighted to ransack for what they could despise is here made important without an evasion or exaggeration," and as "the study of a contemplative nature, of a woman with the sensibility and ambitions of an artist, caught up by her marriage into the life of a public man, Viceroy and Prime Minister, and left, an aged widow, to weigh her achievement and mould her last years to her own pattern."

While both these descriptions are essentially correct, the second probably comes closer to the circumstances from which the idea of the novel sprang. The original conception of Deborah Slane, compelled to sacrifice her artistic aspirations on the altar of her husband's career, was almost certainly inspired by feelings V S-W must herself have experienced a few years earlier, before H.N. had decided to leave the Diplomatic Corps and join the staff of the *Evening Standard.* Deborah Slane did what V S-W had refused to do, but she must at the time have considered the whole question of to what extent a woman was justified in sacrificing her own creative talents to her husband's career. The emancipation of women was still a question of current interest at that time, but V S-W was not a feminist in the ordinary sense of the word. Deborah's thoughts are probably to be interpreted as referring not so much to women in general as to V S-W in particular when she supposed that

> even had she been in love with [Henry], she could see therein no reason for foregoing the whole of her own separate existence. Henry was in love with her, but no one proposed that he should forego his. On the contrary, it appeared that in acquiring her he was merely adding something extra to it. He would continue to lunch with his friends, travel down to his constituency, and spend his evenings at the House of Commons; he would continue to enjoy his free, varied, and masculine life, with no ring upon his finger or difference in his name to indicate the change in his estate; but whenever he felt inclined to come home she must be there, ready to lay down her book, her paper, or her letters; she must be prepared to listen to whatever he had to say; she must entertain his political acquaintances; and even if he beckoned her across the world she must follow. . . . But where, in such a programme, was there room for a studio?

At least one of the grievances mentioned in this extract, the fact that a married woman has to adopt her husband's name for all official purposes, will be recognized as being one of the characteristic features of V S-W's nature.

THE YEAR 1931 WAS also the year in which H.N. made his first, brief, appearance in politics—as a member of Sir Oswald Mosley's New Party and editor of its short-lived newspaper *Action.* V S-W thought the whole venture insane.

Politics was the one field in which there was open disagreement between H.N. and V S-W. This is true both of 1931, and, even more, of 1935, when H.N. stood for election as National Labour candidate for West Leicester. He had hoped to enlist her active support during his election campaign, at least to the extent of her sitting on his platform once or twice during his speeches. However, V S-W refused pointblank to have anything to do with the electioneering. This led to a certain amount of accusation and recrimination, but it had all passed over before polling day, when H.N. was returned to Westminster. A brief account of this incident is to be found in H.N.'s diaries.

It is quite possibly because of the unsuccessful venture of 1931 that politics creep into V S-W's novel *Family History.* Miles Vane-Merrick, the brilliant young politician in the story, would appear to be a combination of the personality of H.N. and the political and economic theories of Maynard Keynes—also a sympathizer with Mosley's New Party for a short time—and his home in Kent bears a remarkable similarity to Sissinghurst Castle. One of the themes of the book—Evelyn's inability to comprehend, other than in an abstract manner, the importance to Miles of his political work—may very well also have been inspired by the differences between V S-W and H.N. caused by almost exactly the same circumstances.

The main theme of the story is the love affair between two people from entirely different social backgrounds. Evelyn Jarrold comes from the Victorian middle class, and has married into a *nouveau riche* family of similar origins and outlook. Miles Vane-Merrick, on the other hand, is of the landed gentry; furthermore he is an intellectual who has espoused the cause of the Labour Party, which he represents in Parliament. Around this central situation V S-W has constructed a framework of social contrasts to illustrate her ideas. At one extreme there is the fast set of the aristocracy, here, as in *The Edwardians,* represented by Sebastian's mother and the Roehamptons. This enables V S-W to comment, through the mouth of Ruth Jarrold, on "the English upper classes (a horrid expression, but she must define them somehow)":

> They looked as though for generations they had been well fed, well warmed, well exercised, and nourished in the conviction that the world could not produce their peers. The standard of looks was amazing; they had the distinction and beauty of thoroughbred animals. The young men were as elegant as greyhounds, the young women coloured as a herbaceous border. What did it matter, Ruth would have added, had she thought of it, that those sleek heads contained no more brains than a greyhound's, since those slender bodies expressed an equal grace? What did it matter that their code should strangely enough involve a contempt for the intellectual advantages which might have been theirs? What did it matter that they should immure themselves within the double barricade of their class and their nationality?

At the other extreme is the middle-class morality of the Jarrolds, who "believe in reputation and in respectability and in keeping up appearances." Here one must make an exception for old Mr. Jarrold, who, despite his millions, remains at heart the unspoiled working-man he has always been.

Both extremes are equally sterile in their way. However, redemption is offered through the Antequils and through those intellectuals, such as Miles Vane-Merrick and Dan, the young heir to the Jarrold empire, who have been influenced by the Antequils' outlook on life.

Although the book has sterling qualities—"She begins with a splendid Thackerayan description of her chief people; she ends with a poignantly tragic account of Evelyn's death"—there is a great deal of truth in the criticism that "there are moments when *Family History* threatens to become less a novel than a tract. Its interest is almost equally divided between the romance and the thesis, and, unfortunately, there is no very strong or necessary connection between the two. For Evelyn Jarrold and her lover are separated, in the end, more by reason of the disparity of their ages than of their backgrounds and ideals."

V S-W published one other book in 1932, a collection of short stories entitled *Thirty Clocks Strike the Hour*. Except for the title story, "The Poet," and "Pomodoro," all the stories in the volume had already been published separately in various magazines in Great Britain.

The story entitled "The Poet" is interesting for the light it casts upon one aspect of the relationship between V S-W and her poetry. The story is about a consumptive young poet, living in Italy, who tells a compatriot he has met there that he is convinced that some, at least, of the poetry he has hammered out with such care is truly great, and will one day make his name immortal. When, after the poet's death a few weeks later, the Englishman goes through his papers in order to rescue these masterpieces for posterity, he finds that the poems really are of the highest quality, as the poet had told him that they were. What he has arrived at, after endless trial and error, are almost word for word copies of some of the most famous poems in the English language.

The inspiration for this story is almost certainly to be found in an experience V S-W had had. Twelve years after the publication of "The Poet," H.N. had occasion to mention to V S-W that the poet Edward Shanks, with whom he had recently had a conversation, complained that he was unable to remember whether a line of poetry was one of his own, or something that he had read years before. To this V S-W replied:

> As to remembering whether a line is by me or by someone else, you know very well that I never could. The first shock of this realisation came when I very laboriously hammered out a line, choosing every word most carefully, and arrived at:
>   "Men are but children of a larger growth."
> Since then I have been cautious.

In itself, this is perhaps not so remarkable; other poets besides Shanks and V S-W have probably had similar experiences. There is, however, an interesting sequel.

In the summer of 1949, the *Poetry Review* asked V S-W if she could let them have some unpublished verses for their jubilee number. She looked through her MSS Book and sent them a poem entitled "The Novice to Her Lover," which she had written in late 1942 or early 1943. Shortly after the poem had appeared in 1949, V S-W discovered that Clifford Dyment had published an almost identical poem entitled "Saint Augustine at 32" in 1943 and had later reprinted it in a book of collected poems. The discovery led to an interesting exchange of letters which was published in the *New Statesman and Nation*. V S-W considers it "unthinkable that either I or Mr. Dyment should have 'lifted' a poem from one another. That supposition can be dismissed." So, of course, it can, if by "lifted" she means "consciously lifted." In view of the remarkable resemblance, both in words and in meter, that the two poems bear to one another, and in view of V S-W's avowed inability to remember what lines are hers and what lines were written by somebody else, there can hardly be much doubt that, subsconsciously, she had been strongly influenced by a memory of the poem which she had probably read in the *St. Martin's Review* in January 1943.

THE FIRST THREE MONTHS OF 1933 saw H.N. and V S-W on a lecture tour of the United States. They lectured, separately and together, all over the country and the tour was, by all accounts, extremely successful. How V S-W herself experienced the tour is shown in a letter she wrote to H.N.:

> I think it is very good for you and me to have to come to America. I am glad we did. I am getting a lot out of it. There may be moments when we are tired and nauseated and bored. But on the whole it is infinitely valuable.

If this is not enthusiastic, it is at least positive. Indeed, she never seems to have been as averse to America and Americans as H.N. obviously was. The more spectacular scenery, such as Niagara Falls and the Grand Canyon, made a great impression on her, but she found that "with all their kindness, these people have very little imagination." The cities, in particular, filled her with dismay:

> Earth and not pavement lay beneath my feet;
> The anger of a dozen rushing brooks
> Replaced the clamour of a city street
> And vapid endless talk of books, books, books.

The immediate literary results of V S-W's visit to the United States were three poems published in her *Collected Poems* the same autumn, as well as one which she never published. Nine years later, she was to write *Grand Canyon*. The view of America that she gives in this book corresponds, by and large, to the one she appears to have held in 1933, except that the portrayal of an average American family is presented in a less flattering light than one would have expected.

> The Driscolls' house resembles all the other houses set along that road. They would not like it to differ in any way. They have lived in it for thirty years and are satisfied with it, though I would not say that they have ever thought of it otherwise than as a convenient and suitable residence. It stands exposed to the glances of passers-by on the road, and to the gaze of the neighbours on either side, but it has never occurred to the Driscolls any more than it has ever occurred to anyone else in the village that privacy might be secured by the planting of a hedge or the erection of a fence. Such things are not done, nor have the Driscolls any wish to do them. Life is pure and open and democratic, so pure as to be almost meaningless, so democratic as to be almost communal. . . . Mr. Driscoll is . . . obviously a man of the utmost rectitude and probity. In business, of course, he would not hesitate to get the better of a weaker rival, would not hesitate to take advantage of someone else's mistake, but in no way would he consider this a departure from the high moral standard of his private life. Possibly this is because he has never thought about it; possibly because in business, as in private life, he accepts other people's standards as he finds them, ready made.

Collected Poems appeared in late 1933. Besides *The Land,* "Sissinghurst," and many of the poems which had been published in *Constantinople, Poems of West and East, Orchard and Vineyard,* and *King's Daughter,* it contained twenty-three poems previously published only in newspapers or periodicals, and thirty-five poems that had not been printed before at all.

The appearance of a volume of poems with this title naturally led some critics to sum up V S-W's position in poetry. Richard Church commented that "this collection of poems has a double interest: first, its beauty, and, secondly, its historical position. Unified and complete, it stands like a frontier tower on the border of a land that we are leaving behind. That land is the England which is vanishing; the England of a ripe and comely rural civilisation which has been sung by Crabbe, Cowper, Thomson, Gray, Tennyson, Hardy, Bridges, and Blunden."

EARLY IN 1934, IN JANUARY, V S-W and Gwen St. Aubyn, H.N.'s sister, went to Portofino, where they took a short lease of the Castello, over-

looking the harbor. In February, accompanied this time by H.N., they
went to Morocco for a month before returning to Sissinghurst. In the
autumn, V S-W published *The Dark Island,* dedicated to Gwen St.
Aubyn.

Of all V S-W's books, none has been received with such wide differences of opinion as this. The *Times Literary Supplement* wrote:

> *The Dark Island,* a work of fervid and disciplined imagination, is
> concerned chiefly with the life of Shirin le Breton, a woman who
> becomes real to us almost by the very improbabilities of her char-
> acter, or by the way in which the author, forcing us to assume her
> premises, convinces us of her conclusions. . . . This would be a
> moving and very exciting story in any hands, but it takes the skill
> of an accomplished writer to make it a work of art as well.

The *New York Times* was equally positive, as was the *Manchester Guardian.* The *New Statesman and Nation* admitted that the book had great
merits, but added "if only Miss Sackville-West had refused all compromise with a superficial plausibility it might have had in it something of greatness." Leonard Woolf had "grave doubts . . . about *The
Dark Island,*" and H.N. wrote in a letter to V S-W:

> Darling, I am sorry I don't like *The Dark Island.* But then if I just
> said I liked all your books, it would detract from the ones I do
> like. I think I like *Sissinghurst* the best of anything you have ever
> written—but that may be personal. But I think nonetheless that it
> *is* the best you have ever written. Then *The Land.* Then *Knole.*
> Then Lady Anne [*The Diary of Lady Anne Clifford*]. Then Mar-
> vell. Then *Challenge.* Then *Heritage.* Then Dragon [*The Dragon in
> Shallow Waters*]. Then G.W. [*Grey Wethers*]. Then *The Heir.*
> Then King's Daughter. Then A.P.S. [*All Passion Spent*]. Then
> *The Edwardians.* . . . thenthedarkisland. I cannot judge of the
> two Persian books since they mean so much to me, but I think I
> should put them after Lady Anne. I think I should put *Family
> History* after the Dragon. Thus you see, I put *The Edwardians* and
> this book last on the list.

Two interrelated aspects of V S-W's character are illustrated
more clearly in *The Dark Island* than in any other of her books—her
arrogance, and the streak of cruelty that one had already guessed at
in *The Dragon in Shallow Waters* and other books. These two traits are
especially noticeable in the manner in which the character of Venn is

handled. It is the atmosphere created in the description of several incidents which shows that these traits are not merely reflections of tendencies inherent in the characters portrayed. As examples may be taken Venn's arrogant treatment of his grandmother, his acquaintances, and above all, of Shirin, when he discovers that it is Storn she loves, not him, and the cruelty of the unpleasant, sadistic little incident when he whips the naked Shirin in Andromeda's Cave.

Leonard Woolf, an acute observer of such characteristics, comments:

> There was a curious and very attractive contradiction in Vita's character. She was then literally—and so few people are literally—in the prime of life, an animal at the height of its powers, a beautiful flower in full bloom. She was very handsome, dashing, aristocratic, lordly, almost arrogant. In novels, people often "stride" in or out of rooms; until I saw Vita, I was inclined to think that they did this only in the unreal, romantic drawing-rooms of the novelist—but Vita really did stride or seem to stride.
>
> To be driven by Vita on a summer's afternoon at the height of the season through the London traffic—she was a very good, but rather flamboyant driver—and to hear her put an aggressive taxi driver in his place, even when she was in the wrong, made one recognize a note in her voice that Sackvilles and Buckhursts were using to serfs in Kent 600 years ago, or even in Normandy 300 years before that. She belonged indeed to a world which was completely different from ours, and the long line of Sackvilles, Dorsets, De La Warrs, and Knole with its 365 rooms had put into her mind and heart an ingredient which was alien to us and at first made intimacy difficult.

Later, when he had got to know V S-W better, he wrote:

> Vita was in many ways an extremely unassuming and modest person, but below the surface, and not so very much below, she had the instinctive arrogance of the aristocrat of the ancient regime, and above the surface she was keenly conscious of the long line of her ancestors, the Sackvilles, Buckhursts, and Dorsets, and of the great house of Knole a few miles away in Kent.

The Dark Island is, to some extent at least, a *roman à clef*. Shirin is a slightly romanticized version of Gwen St. Aubyn (later Lady St. Levan), to whom the book is dedicated, although she has been given several of V S-W's own characteristic traits. Cristina represents another side of V S-W's personality, while Storn, the dark island, is directly modeled on the St. Levans' ancestral home, St. Michael's Mount in Cornwall, which, according to Lady St. Levan, provided the original impulse to write the book. On the other hand Venn le Breton is not a portrait of Lord St. Levan, "who is quite a different sort of man" according to Nigel Nicolson.

It is a complex story that the book relates. One of the themes it explores is masculine jealousy—a subject which V S-W returned to several times. Venn is passionately in love with Storn, just as V S-W was with Knole. When he realizes on his wedding night that Shirin has married him because she, too, loves Storn, he tells her that one thing has got to be clearly understood between them: Storn is his, not hers, "with a cold and final deliberateness . . . that killed her at the very moment when she was most alive." In her despair she turns to Cristina, who has come to the island as her secretary, and gradually establishes an intimacy with her to replace that which she can never form with her husband. It is clearly not Platonic. Venn, whose desire to own her is merely increased by the knowledge that he can never do so, becomes insanely jealous of Cristina and is finally driven to taking her life in a pretended sailing accident.

The Dark Island is also a study of personal privacy. Shirin is an exceedingly reserved person and is always reluctant to reveal her thoughts and feelings more than is absolutely necessary, even to her most intimate acquaintances. "Already at sixteen she had evolved the guiding principle that it was better to keep your own counsel. Oh, by all means! Revelation invariably brought regret in its train. It was better to be secret, very secret, even though for secrecy you had to pay the price of loneliness. It was better not to let anyone know how much you loved the shadow of a bough on a wall, or a swirl of dead leaves falling past a street-lamp; better not to let anyone know how vividly you retained the memory of a sunrise in Persia, or the chatter of the Persian servants; better, above all, not to let anyone know how much you loved the sea and Port Breton. That inner knowledge which told you that life was cruel, told you also that life, just for mischief, might take away such things if it suspected that you loved them. Loneliness was not so very great a price to pay for such security; she would call it privacy rather than loneliness. And, respecting herself with a kind of savage pride, she esteemed her privacy beyond all her other possessions." The title of the book is applicable not only to Storn; it is equally

St. Michael's Mount, Cornwall.

valid of Shirin, who is also a dark island, and, as the book has an auto-
biographic content, to V S-W herself.

It is not really surprising that this powerful, well-written novel
aroused such widely differing responses for, quite apart from its
tragic ending, it deals, as we have seen, with some of the less pleasant
aspects of human behavior. There is also, running beneath the surface of the story, an unmistakable erotic quality, at times openly presented in symbolic form, as in the game of "It" played by Venn,
Shirin, and Cristina; at times, however, covertly, perhaps uninten-
tionally, displayed, and therefore more disturbing. In the latter case it
is also far more difficult to define, being more a fleeting impression
than something that can be pinned down in words, but it will perhaps
be sensed here and there in the passage where Mrs. Jolly gives Shirin
a massage, or in the undertow of emotion that runs between Shirin
and Cristina in Part III of the book. It is a brilliant, but not a comfortable, novel.

NINETEEN THIRTY-FIVE WAS a rather uneventful year for V S-W. H.N.
was in America during the first part of the year to continue work on
the biography of Dwight Morrow that he had begun the previous au-

tumn. In April he was back in Europe and he, V S-W, and Nigel
Nicolson went on a cruise to Greece. In January 1936, Lady Sackville
died at Brighton. One consequence of her death was that the terms of
her will brought the Nicolsons financial security and independence
for the first time since their marriage, as she left V S-W a considerable
sum of money. Up to this time they had, as Nigel Nicolson points out,
been living a very hand-to-mouth existence and had taken a good few
financial risks.

In the autumn of 1935, V S-W had started work on her next
book, which was to be a study of the life of Jeanne d'Arc. *Saint Joan of
Arc* proved to be a biography on a scale very different to that on which
she had written her two previous essays in this genre; in neither of
those works had she penetrated so deeply into the subject of the biography as she did in the life of Jeanne d'Arc. This is possible because
her reasons for choosing Mrs. Behn and Marvell were of a less urgent
nature; her main interest in them appears to have been certain
aspects of their writing. Her choice of a saint for the new book, on the
other hand, was probably governed by a far deeper emotion: the need
to examine her own attitude to religion, and to clarify her mind on
certain religious questions. The reason why the saint chosen was Saint
Joan seems to be that in her V S-W found problems that were similar
to those which she was interested in finding a solution to. The book
entailed a good deal of reading, research, and thought on her part,
and in October 1935 it had taken her, accompanied by Gwen St.
Aubyn, to Domrémy, Chinon, and Orleans. The resulting work was,
in the words of the *Times Literary Supplement,* "a new interpretation."
The review went on:

> Patience, intuition and wide reading have made her completely at
> home. . . . It appears that she has deliberately set herself to
> avoid emotion and to write in a sober, even at times a pedestrian,
> strain. The effect is at first a little disappointing, but as we settle
> down to a book which it is very difficult to stop reading we appre-
> ciate more and more the biographer's method. Not only are the
> events narrated with admirable clarity; the portrait that emerges
> is as impressive as it is satisfactory and the speculation intelligent,
> if cautious. Caution itself is a merit here; and one is indeed grate-
> ful to Miss Sackville-West for not proclaiming that she is the
> inspired solver of the great mystery.

As we shall see, there is clear evidence that during the years from
1936 to 1945 V S-W was much concerned with religious questions, to

which she was endeavoring to find an answer which would have meaning for her personally. The volume of poetry she published in 1938, *Solitude,* has as its central themes death and religion, motifs that are also to be found in *The Garden.* In 1943 she published *The Eagle and the Dove,* comparing the lives of two saints very different from each other in every way: Saint Teresa of Avila and Saint Thérèse of Lisieux. In *Saint Joan of Arc* it is the question of miracles and other supernatural phenomena on which she has to make up her mind.

She defines herself as being

> not what is called a "religious" person in the orthodox sense of the phrase, nor yet a practising member of any organized Church. I do, however, confronted with the ultimate enigma, believe, and believe deeply, in some mysterious central originating force which the natural weakness and insufficiency of human nature finds it necessary to symbolize in a name, an amalgam of fear and comfort, which you may call God or Gott or Dieu or Jah or Allah or X, or even "a pure mathematician," without any reason *necessarily* to identify that force with our own human conceptions of good and evil. It follows logically that, holding this belief, I share with my fellow-mortals the ancient superstition which no scientific explanation can destroy, but which no scientific explanation has as yet been able to account for: the belief in what we conveniently call the supernatural. I believe in it so profoundly as to quarrel with the expressions supernatural or extra-natural. For me there is only one comprehensive, stupendous unity of which we apprehend but the smallest segment.

For many of Jeanne d'Arc's miracles, for example the famous "King's secret," and her ability to pick out the disguised Dauphin from among his courtiers, V S-W attempts to find a natural explanation. In those cases where she is unable to find one that satisfies her, Jeanne's "Voices" for example, she confesses she is "in the unfortunate position of anybody torn between an instinctive reliance on instinct, and a reasonable reliance on reason." She determines to keep an open mind about them in the belief that the future may be able to provide a scientific explanation to what, at present, must be taken on faith.

DURING THE EARLY MONTHS of 1937 both the Nicolsons were away, H.N. on a Government Commission to the African colonies to report on education, and V S-W, with Gwen St. Aubyn, on a tour of Algeria and Morocco. They all returned to Sissinghurst in March, when V S-W settled down to write *Pepita*. From the critics' point of view it was probably the most successful of her books, the response being almost universally positive. The fantastic nature of this true story fascinated them, and they particularly praised V S-W for the great candor, great understanding, and great love with which she had described her mother, of whom she had drawn an enduring portrait, firm in its lines, but profuse in detail of exquisite comedy, hiding little but explaining much. There were a few acute critics, notably A. G. Macdonell in the *Observer* and R. M. in the *New Statesman and Nation*, who surmised that Lady Sackville must have been a far more distressing mother than the book suggested.

During the years between 1934 and 1947 V S-W did not produce much fiction. In Leonard Woolf's opinion, "the springs of Vita's invention and imagination which she required for novel writing began to run dry." He had had grave doubts about *Family History* and *The Dark Island,* and after *Pepita*

> she brought us the manuscript of a novel which we felt we could not publish. . . . Vita was an ideal author from the publisher's point of view; she never complained when things went wrong and was extraordinarily appreciative of the publisher if they went right. This made it all the more unpleasant to have to tell her that we thought her novel not good enough for us to publish. We knew, too, that we should lose her as an author, because there were many reputable publishers who would publish this novel in order to get her "on their list."

The novel was *Grand Canyon,* which Michael Joseph published in November 1942. Interior evidence shows that the book must have been written after the fall of France in 1940, and if V S-W followed her normal practice, it was written in the twelve months preceding its publication, that is to say not long after Virginia Woolf had committed suicide in March 1941. V S-W was feeling rather depressed at the time, and Virginia Woolf's death was naturally a great shock to her. Whatever the reason, *Grand Canyon* is a book that fails to live up to its promises in several respects. The Author's Note states that it is intended to be a cautionary tale, a warning to the U.S.A. not to be deceived by Nazi propaganda, but although one of the characters is a Nazi agent, and although Germany launches a surprise attack on

America, these things are not felt to be essential to the story, their only function being to create a feeling of tension and to provide a credible reason for the death of a large number of people: a natural catastrophe would have served her purpose equally well. The story begins as a study of a group of people staying at an isolated hotel and their reactions to each other. Halfway through, the book turns into a piece of science fiction concerned with questions of good and evil, for the residents, having been evacuated from the burning hotel, continue their lives on the floor of the Grand Canyon without realizing that they were all killed by a bomb on their way down. The sudden and unannounced change of direction is confusing. So is the fact that there are in the story characters and incidents which one feels must have been introduced for some special purpose, but which, in the end, prove to have either no particular significance, or one that is quite different from what one had anticipated. To take an example: in a novel which is concerned with communication, as the first part of *Grand Canyon* is, the presence of a blind man and a deaf man will inevitably be understood as having some symbolic importance. So they have, but their function is not at all what one had expected; one of the ways in which the other characters are brought to realize that they are all dead is when they gradually notice that the blind man can see again and the deaf man hear.

Leonard Woolf was quite right when he surmised that V S-W's books would no longer be published by the Hogarth Press. She had begun by publishing her poetry with John Lane, The Bodley Head, and her fiction with Collins until she had transferred to Heinemann's in 1922. Virginia Woolf had recruited her for the Hogarth Press in 1924 and, apart from *The Land,* which she had probably already promised to Heinemann's, and a few minor works, she had remained with the Hogarth Press until Virginia Woolf's death. Michael Joseph, to whom V S-W then transferred, was her publisher until her own death in 1962.

FROM 1937 UNTIL the end of the period covered by this chapter, that is up to the end of 1946, V S-W's life seems to have been outwardly uneventful. Immediately after the publication of *Pepita,* she and Gwen St. Aubyn spent some weeks in the south of France, and it was during this time that she conceived the idea of writing *The Eagle and the Dove* and *Solitude.* Apart from this, she went abroad little more before the outbreak of war.

Harold Nicolson, 1946.

H.N. was fully occupied by politics during these years; it was with the deterioration of the international situation that his knowledge of foreign affairs proved an asset to the House of Commons. He was in London for the greater part of every week, returning to Sissinghurst only at weekends, and not always then. V S-W, on the other hand, spent most of her time in Kent.

Inwardly, however, it would seem that these years were, for V S-W, not so calm and uneventful as they might have appeared on the surface. *Solitude*, the poem she published in 1938, is filled with signs of spiritual unrest. The introductory poem, "Rocamadour," dedicated to Gwen St. Aubyn, states:

> So, rightly, you divined
> That I within the trouble of my mind
> Would in Rocamadour a refuge find.
>   . . .
> How did you know that I was worldly-sick?
> Because you knew, I dedicate this verse
> To you for better or for worse.

The poem itself moves from the initial apparent optimism of

> —but who would sleep when he might wake? . . .
> Wring the last midnight minute to its end?

—an optimism that has a slight feeling of defiance about it—to the
deeply pessimistic

> —but who would wake when he might sleep?
> Who live, when he might die? . . .
> Who would not rather, in this world of sin,
> Sleep in forgetfulness? choose sleep and death.

Leading up to this conclusion, V S-W gives a brief summary of the experiences of the spirit, of moods and outlooks, of "this tender hell of
passion, love, tradition, closing jaws," of days when one was "dull,
muted, sealed," of other days filled with happiness, "What gaiety,
what joy, what faith extreme."

But at her back she always hears a whisper that urges:

> Hurry on!
> No time for admiration of the swan,
> No time for balance and comparison,
> Time only for the scrambling jettison
> To save a labouring ship.
> The port is Death; oh, hurry, hurry on!

Faced with the thought of death, with the necessity of yielding her
further keeping "into such hands as planned this intricate I," she feels
obliged to add:

> And since I know not what those hands may be
> I ask not whence? nor whether? nor yet why?
> I only know, not sadly, but resigned,
> That in the humour of a master-mind
> This name, this I, this label must be torn,
> Scrapped with the implications that were me.

It is true she says she is resigned to her fate. Furthermore, she goes on
to say that she scorns religious consolation, and boasts:

> No Church I need; I seek my God direct,
> Knowing myself unchosen, unelect.

But, in reality, this is a pose, a device to bolster up her morale by pretending to a courage that she does not actually possess. At heart she is appalled, and feels the need of reassurance. She cries:

> Give us a sign. Regard, O God, our need.
> Give us a sign. We die without your heed.

There comes no sign:

> But silence meets me; all my prayer is vain.

The dilemma for her is that she is unable to find by ratiocination any answer to the problems that beset her, and incapable by nature of accepting the answer which satisfies:

> . . . that happy, enviable soul
> Greeting the great solution of our doubt
> Simply, to take it all-embracing, whole,
> A charmèd circle, leaving us without.

Hence the tragic feelings with which the poem ends.

There is one point of particular interest in the poem. When asking God for a sign to be given, V S-W singles out one aspect of her doubts as being of central significance, the key to all the problems confronting her, and puts it in the form of a concrete question, which it might be illuminating to consider:

> We only ask to learn if you will teach
> Class by enormous class, or each by each.

The most obvious interpretation of the question is that it asks whether knowledge of God's purpose will be revealed through the Church, or by individual enlightenment. If this is indeed what it means, it gives us a clear indication of the reason why V S-W was interested in hagiology in general, and in Jeanne d'Arc in particular. It was Jeanne's locutions that attracted her; were they indeed of God, or did they admit of some more mundane explanation?

If V S-W's interest in Jeanne d'Arc was primarily because she felt the need to form some opinion of the nature of Jeanne's locutions, it seems very likely that one of the reasons for her interest in Saint Teresa of Avila was that, as regards background, temperament, and some other features, she and Saint Teresa appeared to have a great deal in common.

Teresa de Cepeda Dávila y Ahumada, one of the subjects of *The Eagle and the Dove,* was of noble birth. She had received an ordinary aristocratic upbringing and had never, as a child, had the least thought of devoting herself to the religious life. Her entry, as a pupil, not as a postulant, into the convent of Santa Maria de Gracia at the age of sixteen was imposed upon her from the outside; apparently the result of the discovery of a Lesbian relationship between her, a cousin, and another girl. Although originally hostile to the idea of becoming a nun, feelings of guilt and a fear of Hell persuaded her to enter a convent and eventually to take the veil. It was not until thirty years later, when she was in her fifties, that she began what was her real life work; the reformation of the Carmelite order in Spain.

She was a woman of immense practical common sense and strength of character, "one of the most capable women the world has seen," as indeed she needed to be to deal with "shrewd men, suspicious prelates, and jealous organisations." And, adds V S-W, "the reader who chooses to pick his way through the tangle recorded in the documents is left wondering not only at the dissentions and treacheries of the men of God but also at the stature of the woman steering amongst them." But Saint Teresa was much more than an able administrator; she was a writer and, above all, a mystic. V S-W appreciated the writer for her clear, energetic, even homely prose, but also for the fact that "in addition to this factual, often of-the-soil vividness of expression, she possessed also something of the poet's vision, when her imagery flamed more splendid"; it is, however, Saint Teresa the mystic who is the focus of V S-W's interest.

The mystic and the poet have much in common. In the first place, both are faced with the problem, even more difficult for the mystic than the poet, of explaining their visions in ordinary language:

> The mystics themselves have dwelt on the hopelessness of the attempt to translate their experiences into intelligible words. Like the poet, they must take refuge in symbol and metaphor, more potent than dry affirmation, more evocative than statement.

Secondly, and this is perhaps the essential feature for V S-W, there is the question of inspiration and vision. "We may well believe that the condition of the artist in moments of creative inspiration, the 'fine frenzy,' is closely comparable to the rapture of the mystic; that the two experiences, in fact, are similar in their nature though perhaps not consciously in their aim." Later she expands this statement, adding:

> for there is a greater resemblance between the creative artist and the mystic than between any other brands of human beings . . . that sense of being lifted out of self, exalted, filled with power, filled with a perception not blinding but revealing—it must never be forgotten that the aim is not consciously similar, not similar even in retrospect; unless, indeed, the pursuit of beauty runs a parallel path to the pursuit of God. As well it may.

While it is not difficult to see what it was that attracted V S-W's interest to Saint Teresa of Avila, it does not at first seem quite so clear what there was about Saint Thérèse of Lisieux that made V S-W choose her as the second saint for this "Study in Contrasts," as the subtitle of the book calls it. The idea of writing *The Eagle and the Dove* first came to V S-W in 1937, while she and her sister-in-law, Gwen St. Aubyn, were motoring through the south of France. V S-W evidently told H.N. of her intention, for in October he wrote to her mentioning St. Thérèse of Lisieux. This letter has been printed in *Diaries and Letters, 1930–39* with the addition of a footnote stating that "V. S-W had just conceived the idea of writing *The Eagle and the Dove*." Although the idea came to her then, it seems that she did not actually write the book until several years later, for the acknowledgements mention the fact that it was written under war-time conditions.

In an article written in 1950 about one of her poems, V S-W states that "I wrote my poem 'The Novice to Her Lover' some time in 1942 or early in 1943, when I was engaged on an essay about St. Thérèse of Lisieux, the 'novice' that I had in mind." She sent the poem to "a recently converted Catholic and a devotee of St. Thérèse . . . embodied in a letter." It seems almost certain that the person referred to was Gwen St. Aubyn. The latter was a convert and lived nearby in a house in Sissinghurst during the early years of the war. It therefore seems likely that V S-W's interest in St. Thérèse was aroused by her sister-in-law and that, contrary to what might have been supposed, it was with this saint that V S-W was originally concerned, St. Teresa of Avila, with whom she would have been far more in sympathy, being added later.

There can be little doubt that there were problems of a religious nature on V S-W's mind about this time. After the publication of *The*

Eagle and the Dove there was a widespread rumor that she was about to become a Roman Catholic. She denied it. One cannot, however, escape being aware of the fact that she had devoted very serious thought to the question. *Saint Joan of Arc,* 1936, *Solitude,* 1938, and *The Eagle and the Dove,* 1943, show a progressively deeper concern for and a greater knowledge of religious, especially Catholic, problems. The last of these books in particular could not have been written without undertaking a considerable amount of study of the dogma of the Church. Though by no means uncritical of certain aspects of Catholicism, such as the question of relics, the underlying tone of the book as a whole bespeaks a basic acceptance of the spirit of the Roman Catholic Church which indicates that the writer is, to say the least, positively disposed toward it:

> The roaring of the crowd was silenced only by the command to stand while Peter should speak through the lips of Pius. Strange, awesome ritual of this Church with all its hierarchy, tradition, power, splendour and organisation, so self-contained within the framework of the temporal realms of this world, so immutable, so secret in its workings among the hearts of millions, so apparent in its majesty on such occasions of affirmation in its Roman stronghold!

As we saw in *Solitude,* V S-W seems to have had a strong desire to be able to believe, and envied those who were capable, by a simple act of faith, of cutting straight through to the heart of those questions which were problems to her. *Solitude* also indicates that she thought that there were two possible paths which might lead her to belief: the teaching of the Church, on one hand, and revelation on the other. She had studied the revelations of one saint and the mysticism of two others, presumably in order to find out what she could learn from their experiences. It is, of course, not possible to come to any conclusion about what she decided in her own mind, but it is clear that several years of speculation and study had brought her to a position in which the Catholic Church exercised a certain attraction on her. It would have been reasonable to expect her to continue to study Catholicism and to deepen her knowledge of the Church still further, in which case probably no one would have been surprised if she had eventually been received into the Roman Catholic Church. But she does not.

To move from *The Eagle and the Dove* to *The Garden* is to enter a

different world. In form the poem is a parallel to *The Land,* doing for
gardening what the latter did for agriculture, but it is far more in-
trospective than the earlier poem, and far more pessimistic. Here
there is none of the hopefulness in tone and outlook that characterized the life of the two saints; instead there is the realization that life
has slipped away without her knowing it, that time is running out:

> Oh Days, be double! Hours, be forty-eight!
>   . . .
> Oh bolting Time, rough pony of my days,
> Halt by the hedgerow of my life to graze.
>   . . .
> Oh years gone by! oh years still going past
> In wild crescendo, fast and ever fast
> Like some mad back-cloth scenes that, worked at speed,
> Drawn backwards in their prospect still recede,
> And I, of God! not ready yet to live.

There is also "the horrible loneliness of the soul":

> For our life is terribly private in the end,
> In the last resort;
> And if our self's a stranger, what's a friend?
> A pretty children's game of let's pretend!
> We can share nor the puzzle nor the grief,
> Neither the physical nor the mental pain,
> The insecurity, the fears insane . . .
> How fortunate, that life should be so brief!

Deeply disturbed by these feelings, V S-W turns once again to religion, but this time she does not seek an answer in the lives of saints;
nor does she consider the doctrines of Rome. On the contrary, we
find her rejecting these doctrines, regretting that the Church has ob-
scured the simple teachings of Christ with a heavy layer of dogma:

> Truths surrounded Him at His birth
> When He first drew breath;
> Such plain and pastoral truths of the barn and the earth.
>   . . .
> Great St. Peter and great St. Paul
> Travelled far from the stable stall.
> Cathedrals, cardinals, all the state,
> All the dogma and all the weight,

All the structure of Church and creed,
When Christ in His greater simplicity
Had already given us all we need.

This is a very different attitude toward the Church than that displayed in *The Eagle and the Dove*. But the difference goes even deeper.
V S-W not only had a great love of nature; she also knew a great deal
about it and could not help being struck by the discrepancies she noticed between Christianity and nature:

—Christ would have said that bird to bird was brother,
But Christ and Nature seldom speak alike.

To her, God and nature were much more intimately associated and,
being unable to reconcile the teachings of Christianity with the evidence of her senses, she now tends to rely more on the latter, with the
result that a clearly marked pantheistic outlook appears in her poetry:

Then in the poignant moment made aware
We are all things, the flower and the tree,
Detail of petal, and the general burst
Greening the valley and th'horizon hurst;
The bud still folded and the bud fulfilled;
We are the distant landscape and the near.
We are the drought, we are the dew distilled;
The saturated land, the land athirst;
We are the day, the night, the light, the dark;
The water-drop, the stream; the meadow and the lark.
We are the picture, and the hand that paints;
The trodden pathway, and the foot that trod;
We are the humble echo of great saints
Who knew that God was all and all was God.

An unpublished poem of a very similar nature, presumably written
about the same time, will be found on pages 152–53. Apparent, too,
are reflections which are based on neo-platonic concepts:

There is another world that doubles this poor world,
Where intimations like a source, a stream
Sprung from a rock by bolt of vision cleft
Crowd on the spirit in an hour too brief
But in its stab, extreme.

The conclusion she reaches in the lyric in which she implores time to slow down his headlong flight for a while is that there is no hereafter:

> Halt, and consider as you wildly go:
>
>   . . .
>
> My extant life my only episode;
> Your rattling course completes my only road.

The Eagle and the Dove was published at the beginning of November 1943; the first lines of *The Garden* were written on January 3, 1944. During the few months which passed between the completion of one and the beginning of the other V S-W's attitude to religion underwent a radical change. Catholicism loses its attraction, and instead she develops an interest in pantheism and neo-platonism. The exact reason for this sudden and rather surprising change must, of course, remain a matter of conjecture. There are, however, good grounds for believing that it was due to the break-up of an intimate relationship with a close friend, probably a Catholic, due to the latter's religious convictions, as the following lines from an unpublished poem entitled "Requiem" seem to show.

> I had not thought that you who shared
> My days, my nights, my heart, my life,
> Would slash me with a naked knife
> And gently tell me not to bleed
> But to accept your crazy creed.
>
> You speak of God, but you have cut
> The one last thread, as you have shut
> The one last door that open stood
> To show me still the way to God.
> If this be God, this pain, this evil,
> I'd sooner change and try the Devil.
>
>   . . .
>
> You're safe; that's gone, that wild caprice,
> But tell me once before I cease,
> Which does your Church esteem the kinder rôle,
> To kill the body, or destroy the soul?

It seems very likely that this poem was addressed to Gwen St. Aubyn. V S-W's interest in religion dates from the middle of the 1930's, and

And; so it ends.
We who were lovers may be friends.
I have some weeks in which to steel
My heart and teach myself to feel
Only a sober tenderness
Where once was passion's loveliness.

I had not thought that there would come
Your touch to make our music dumb,
Your meeting touch upon the string
That still was vibrant, still could sing
When I impatiently might wait
Or parted from you at the gate.

You took me weak and unprepared.
I had not thought that you who shared
My days, my nights, my heart, my life,
Would slash me with a naked knife
And gently tell me not to bleed
But to accept your crazy creed.

You speak of God, but you have cut
The one last thread, as you have shut
The one last door that open stood
To show me still the way to God.
If this be God, this pain, this evil,
I'd sooner change and try the devil.

Darling, I thought of nothing mean;
I thought of killing straight and clean.
You're safe; that's gone, that wild caprice,
But tell me once before I cease,
Which does your Church esteem the kinder role,
To kill the body, or destroy the soul?

Manuscript of the poem "Requiem."

1 line space

Low sinks the sun, and long the shadows fall.
The sun-clock, faithful measurer of time,
Fixed to man's dwelling on his flimsy wall
Or tabled flat on curving pedestal
Amongst his dying flowers, tells the last
Hours of the year (and also of my rhyme.)
Now is the sunlight ebbing, faint and fast
In intermittent gleams that seldom cut
Throughout the day the quadrant of our fate
With the slow stroke that says TOO SOON ... TOO LATE ...
BEWARE, THE OPEN GATE WILL SOON BE SHUT.
The stroke that slowly turns our present to our past.

November sun that latens with our age,
Filching the zest from our young pilgrimage,
Writing old wisdom on our virgin page.
Not the hot ardour of the summer's height,
Not the sharp-minted coinage of the spring
When all was but a delicate delight
And all took wing and all the bells did ring;
Not the spare winter, clothed in black and white,
Forcing us into fancy's eremite,
But gliding time that slid us into gold
Richer and deeper as we grow more old
And see some meaning in this dying day;
Travellers of the year, who still can faintly say
Thank God that beauty walks the common way.

AMEN.

30.10.1945

The last page of *The Garden*.

the dedication of *Solitude* (1938) indicates that it was Gwen St. Aubyn who awakened that interest:

> To G. St. A.
>
>   . . .
> How did you know that I was worldly-sick?
>
> Because you knew, I dedicate this verse
> To you for better or for worse;
> To you, who opened first my shuttered eyes
> To the first difficult and deep surmise.

The publication of *The Garden* marked the end of a period of V S-W's life and authorship; the sources of her poetic inspiration dried up. With the exception of three short poems, none of which was longer than twenty lines, she was to publish no poetry at all after this; if she wrote more, she cannot have considered it worth preserving, for there exists nothing dated after 1946, even in manuscript, except a short farewell poem to a housekeeper who left her service in 1948.

CHAPTER V

⚕ 1947 – 1962 ⚕

V S-W PUBLISHED TWO BOOKS IN 1947: *Nursery Rhymes* and *Devil at Westease*. The first of these is a light piece of work dealing in a humorous manner with the origins and meaning of some well-known English nursery rhymes. The last four pages contain some reflections upon poetry and criticism.

Devil at Westease, which was published only in the United States, hinges upon an extreme case of duality, a true Jekyll and Hyde personality. Although duality is, as we have seen, a motif that occurs in several of her works of fiction, it is treated quite differently in this book. In earlier novels her attitude to duality does not appear to have been a conscious one; it was rather an aspect of personality, possibly unconsciously introduced into the story, which she wished to grapple with and investigate for her own benefit. In *Devil at Westease,* however, the motif is treated quite objectively; the fact that Wyldbore Ryan and Professor Warren are really the same person is the key to the solution of the mystery, as Ryan and Warren provide each other with alibis which collapse when it becomes clear that they are not two separate persons.

Though this objectivity on V S-W's part seems to indicate that she has come to terms with the conception of duality and that it worries her no more, traces of ambivalence still remain. As Ryan appears in the role of Warren for technical reasons only, that is to provide him with an alibi for the murder, he should be perfectly aware of the fact that Warren does not exist. In fact, the way in which Ryan refers to Warren, even when he has admitted that the man is a fiction, gives the

reader the impression that in some way he really does feel that Warren has a life of his own. "I'm no criminal," he retorts when taxed with
the deception, "that was the Professor."

The book is not only a detective story but also demands, both of
the author herself and of her readers, the answer to an ethical question: what are the relative values of the man of creative genius and the
ordinary, nonproductive citizen? Provided that no one else will suffer
if he keeps silent, how should a man act who is the only person to
know that a productive artist of the very highest ability has been guilty
of murdering a man of the people? Should he speak out or not? In
order to pose this question in the framework of the story she has
chosen, V S-W has to reverse the normal Jekyll and Hyde situation,
making Wyldbore Ryan, the amoral man, the basic character, and
Warren, the kindly old professor, merely a role into which Ryan slips
when the mood or occasion arises. Rather courageously V S-W thus
makes the man for whose life she pleads an unsympathetic character,
not a pleasant one. It is some measure of her skill that Beatrice Sher-
man described the book as having a "subtle and original turn of plot,"
and concluded by saying "The solution is fantastic but perfectly fair to
the reader; a satisfactory ending to a puzzler of exceptional charm
and finish."

NINETEEN FORTY-SEVEN marked the beginning of a long period during which V S-W's creative ability seemed to desert her almost entirely. From the middle of 1947 up to the beginning of 1953, more
than five years, she published nothing except a few magazine articles on various subjects. However, in January 1947, she did make a
start on a work of some importance. It was the life of Anne Marie
Louise d'Orleans, Duchesse de Montpensier, 1627–1693—La Grande
Mademoiselle. In spite of the fact that "she isn't *quite* my sort of thing"
there were aspects of her story that V S-W found interesting:

> Her own description of herself is fascinating as a psychological
> document. It is a study in self-delusion by a most sincere person.
> It is on these lines that I shall try to base my portrait of her. You
> see, she persuaded herself that she had no worldly ambition, yet
> spent half her time trying to marry Kings or Emperors, and it was
> only when she fell in love with Lauzun that she came round to
> her own conception of herself as a person without ambition. A
> very interesting character.

However, the book did not progress well, and it appears to have been laid aside soon afterwards, not to be resumed until 1953. It was not finished until 1959, twelve years after it was begun.

FOR H.N. THE END OF THE WAR had meant several changes. He lost his seat in Parliament in the Labour landslide of 1945, and was given notice to leave his chambers in King's Bench Walk the same year; they were required for practicing barristers. In 1946, he had moved his address in London to Neville Terrace, South Kensington, and in February 1947, he joined the Labour Party. He was invited to stand as Labour Candidate in North Croydon in the 1948 by-election. His defeat there was virtually the end of his political career, and after that he devoted most of his time to writing and literature. In 1948, he was invited to write the official biography of King George V. He accepted, and in 1952 completed the life, his magnum opus, for which he received a knighthood in 1953.

IRONICALLY ENOUGH, ALTHOUGH V S-W WAS never to write any more poetry and was temporarily unable to write prose, it was now that honors began to descend on her. True, the value of *The Land* had immediately been recognized and she had been awarded the Hawthornden Prize in 1927; now she was given the Heinemann Prize for *The Garden*. In December 1947, she was made a Companion of Honour for her services to literature. In 1949, she was appointed to the bench as Justice of the Peace at Cranbrook, and the same year took her seat on the National Trust's Gardens Committee and on the Executive of the Society for the Preservation of Rural Kent. She was also invited by the British Council to make lecture tours for them; in February and March 1948, she was in Morocco, Algeria, and Tunisia which, incidentally, provided a neat solution to the difficulty of her nonappearance on the platform during H.N.'s electoral campaign in North Croydon. Then in 1949 she went to Spain, her "half-native land," for the British Council. This was a source of great pleasure to her as she was able to visit places she had written about in *The Eagle and the Dove* and *Pepita*. When, for example, she looked at the list of places she was to visit, she found that she was to lecture on modern English literature at Malaga, she exclaimed, "Now supposing Pepita, as a little *muchacha* in Malaga, could have had a glimpse into the future, and foreseen her granddaughter not as 'a bird in the air' but as a lecturer on a platform,

wouldn't she have been incredulous and surprised? How Virginia
[Woolf] would have appreciated this!"

However, all this recognition was no compensation to her for the
fact that she was unable to write:

> I am really rather depressed by my inability to write the simplest
> thing. No, let me be truthful, I am not "rather depressed," but
> mortally depressed. I am like a motor-car that has been standing
> in a cold garage and refuses to give out even one little *pétard* of a
> firing-spark. I daresay it will warm up again some day, but mean-
> while it is as cold as a frog.

This was in January 1950. In December the same year, however,
she was able to write in quite a different tone:

> Darling, I must write you another little note just to say how happy
> I am writing. It does make the whole difference in life. I just tell
> you this, because I like sharing things with you. I have been so
> miserable in the last two or three years, not being able to write;
> really worried I have been, thinking that it was gone from me for
> ever.

The book that she was working on was *The Easter Party*. But although she had begun to write again, progress was slow judged by her
previous production, for it was not published until January 1953,
more than two years later. This was a considerable time for V S-W to
have spent on a novel of only one hundred and ninety pages when
one considers that *All Passion Spent* and *The Dark Island*, both of about
three hundred pages, were written in about ten months each. When
the book finally appeared in January 1953, it was ridiculed in a sarcastic review by Marghanita Laski:

> After such triumphs of the novelist's art as *The Edwardians* and *All
> Passion Spent*, it must be confessed that Miss Sackville-West's *The
> Easter Party* is disappointing. The story of the eminent Q.C. who
> allows himself neither to feel human affections nor to consum-
> mate his marriage, but is at last brought to his senses through a
> threat to his beloved Alsatian dog seems to lack both the psycho-
> logical probability and (surprisingly in view of Miss Sackville-
> West's previous achievements) a coherent integral shape. There
> are, however, some pleasing and evocative descriptions of gar-
> dens, and a fascinating side-track, unfortunately not fully ex-

plored, in the lovely Lady Quarles, who, when she experiences panic fear, smells goat.

As this review appeared in *The Observer,* the newspaper to which both V S-W and H.N. contributed regularly, and as it was one of the first reviews to be published, it cut deep, more particularly as this was the first book she had been able to write for a long time. V S-W was not, however, the sort of person to give up on meeting the first reverse; she was made of sterner stuff:

> My poor Viti is hurt by a review of her new novel [*The Easter Party*] by Marghanita Laski, which is contemptuous and wounding. When such things occur to me, I become depressed and miserable. But Viti just gets angry, which I suppose is better.

In actual fact, the story of the book is a very complex one which can by no means be dismissed so facilely. The *Times Literary Supplement* showed much greater perspicacity when it pointed out that "something of all the preoccupations of Miss Sackville-West's earlier books has been brought into play, not omitting *The Eagle and the Dove. . . . The Easter Party* is therefore interesting not only in isolation, but as a development of the outlook which produced *The Edwardians.*" After commenting on V S-W's attitude to the English social structure, the review goes on to add that what she is concerned with in the present book is the mental aura of Sir Walter Mortibois, Q.C.:

> It hinges on the character of Sir Walter Mortibois, in whose name certain legal colleagues saw an apt pun: "dead wood." Mortibois, professionally in the thick of the human struggle, is privately wary of emotional entanglements. He is a man who could propose to the woman of his choice, saying, "My heart is in no way engaged." He sought a bargain with her for companionship but not love. Rose, a daughter of the parsonage, accepted, not for money or position, but because, paradoxically, she had fallen in love with him. On their honeymoon in the warm south he lectures her on the heavenly bodies, and that is all that is bodily in their relationship. At this point the reader may ask, is Mortibois human? It is a tribute to Miss Sackville-West's skill that he is credible, even exasperatingly so. His is a complex character, and every facet as presented is in itself credible. . . . We have been presented with a picture of Walter in his room in the small hours of that morning when "his secretive nature loved the privacy and

solitude." We find him reading, of all books, *The Cloud of Unknow-ing,* St. Augustine, St. John of the Cross. To these books, we are told, "he returned over and over again." . . . We now deduce in him something earnestly enquiring, unsatisfied, perhaps self-tor-menting, behind all his logical pessimism and cool detachment. . . . He is still, the reader feels, a character groping after realiza-tion, after reality. This is not to say he does not live here: unreal people are not only those in books.

Near the end of the review comes the observation, "Ultimately what her work poses is a religious question." This is perhaps the key to a full understanding of what V S-W is attempting to express. A careful study of the book brings to light facts which indicate that the theme of the book is similar to that of *The Garden;* the conflict in a soul searching for God, and torn between Christianity on one side and paganism or pantheism on the other. Walter Mortibois is a man in whom "a sense of the suffering and folly of the human race flowed ceaselessly as a burning accompaniment to the blood in his veins. . . . In another age and in another country he might have cho-sen the contemplative life." When the demands of his profession make it necessary for him to take a wife, he seeks out a suitable girl very carefully and, when proposing to her, warns her that "I want my marriage to be a marriage in name alone. You understand what I mean?" He wishes to give her no explanation of his reasons for dic-tating this condition, but adds:

> I can at least assure you of two things; that they are in no way dis-creditable, and that they have no connection with my health. . . . It is merely that I should not prefer to disclose, at present, what is after all only a personal idiosyncrasy but one which is very deeply associated with my private philosophy of life.

He never does tell his wife, but the reader, aware, as Rose is not, of Walter's deep interest in the mystics, and observing phrases used about him, such as "his chosen celibacy," may come to the conclusion that his celibacy has something in common with that of the religious recluse.

It is not, however, quite as simple as that. Juliet, the notorious Lady Quarles, introduces another element into the story. She, who describes herself as old and shop-soiled, is essentially a figure of in-nocence, despite her well-earned reputation. "There was something nymph-like about Juliet, untarnished despite the life she had left and the many hands through which she had passed." The reason is that she stands quite outside Christian morality; "her pantheism instinctive; without effort she identified herself with the pebbles of her brook, the leaf fallen on her path." But she is also the focal point through which Panic powers can manifest themselves, and, as such, a symbol of sexuality. As it is clear that she holds a great fascination for Walter, the Pan motif seems to suggest that his celibacy is not only a voluntary abstinence similar to that of the Christian mystic, but is also connected with a fear of sexuality itself. The strange incident in the grotto, and its sequel, when Walter discovers that the clock in his wife's room has stopped at the precise moment at which the manifestation in the grotto took place, might be taken as being a demonstration to Walter of the strength of the powers with which he will have to contend if he chooses the Christian path.

During a conversation with Walter's brother, Gilbert, an eminent brain surgeon, Rose voices a thought that Juliet had already expressed forcibly to Walter when she said, "Walter darling, have you no heart to protect? Have you never suffered? Are you not afraid that some day you may be called upon to suffer?" Rose also shows Gilbert the weak points in Walter's armor when she says that "there are only two things he cares for: Svend and Anstey"—his dog and his house.

Throughout the book, emphasis is given to the fact that it is Easter time; at various times almost all the principal characters comment pointedly on it, which makes it look as though V S-W wishes to draw the reader's attention to the significance of some aspect of Easter. The most obvious aspect to choose would be redemption through an external agency.

On Easter Day, Gilbert, to whom Rose had said, "You are both practical men, you and Walter, but you, Gilbert, have something Christ-like about you," persuades Walter to hand Svend over to him for an operation which, while being of the greatest value to mankind, will inevitably result in the death of the dog. Now Walter learns what suffering really is.

On Monday night, Rose discovers when she happens to look at the fireplace in the hall that, perhaps thrown off balance by the shock of losing Svend, "for once, Walter must have neglected to pile up the ashes." During the night the house catches fire and is burnt to the ground. But, although Walter has at one blow lost the two things that were dearest in life to him, "he seemed transformed, a different man,

a man suffering a violent form of catharsis, a purging, an experience."

Viewed in this light, *The Easter Party* appears to be an exposition
of the religious and moral problems confronting V S-W, to which an
arbitrary solution has been provided. This solution, which is basically
Christian, appears to be different to the one that would have resulted
from the premises in *The Garden,* which tended to be more pantheistic
than Christian.

Soon after the publication of *The Easter Party,* V S-W resumed
work on *Daughter of France,* which had been laid aside since 1947. "I
revive the idea of writing about La Grande Mademoiselle," she wrote
in her diary in March 1953. She struggled on with the book through
1954 and 1955 although she felt that La Grande Mademoiselle had
begun to dominate her life in an intolerable manner: "The Big Miss
stands behind me with a whip," was the way she felt about it at times.
But progress remained very slow. It was not made quicker by the fact
that she had been suffering from arthritis during these years, and
now, in March 1955, damaged her back in a fall. Then, in the autumn
of 1955, an American, Francis Steegmuller, published his biography
of La Grande Mademoiselle, which received very favorable reviews.
V S-W was greatly distressed, fearing that all her work had been in
vain, and for a time contemplated giving up the book altogether.

About a year after this, in January 1957, V S-W and H.N. went
on the first of the winter cruises they were to make every year after
this up till 1961. They had, for some years before this, been in the
habit of going off together for a month's tour of some country,
usually France or Italy, but sometimes Great Britain. The winter
cruises began to be the time when V S-W did a large part of her writing. The first cruise was to Cape Town, Singapore, and Java. During
the two months they were on board, V S-W managed to write a considerable amount:

> V. has written some 40,000 words of *La Grande Mademoiselle,* but
> does not think she will be able to finish the book by the time we
> get back to England. And then will come all those interruptions
> and the Mademoiselle will be put away into a drawer until the
> long dark autumn evenings come. She does not, I fear, possess
> my gift of concentration, being so polite to those who intrude
> upon her that she becomes distracted . . . her sublime patience
> with dawdlers ends by wearing her down.

The following winter, 1957–1958, saw them on a cruise to the Caribbean, Panama, and the Pacific coast of South America. Not so much was written on this trip, as V S-W was ill for part of the time. However, on 13th August, 1958, she could say:

> Do you know what happened at 9.30 last night? La Grande Mademoiselle died, aged 63. This does not mean that I have not still got a lot to do, but the book is so to speak finished, and another month should clear it up. Ouf!

Nevertheless the book was not published until the end of March the following year. It might be called her magnum opus in prose; none of her other books had taken her anything like so long to write, and for none of her other books did she have to study such quantities of material. As the *Times Literary Supplement* points out:

> Her story is to be found in contemporary sources so copious as to appear positively horrifying. At first glance it would seem that Everybody who was Somebody at the courts of Louis XIII and XIV wrote memoirs, kept a diary or sent off a quantity of letters every week. Mademoiselle herself left a voluminous although patchy autobiography; yet this part of Miss Sackville-West's material is a drop in the ocean of personal records provided by courtiers, priests, valets, ladies-in-waiting, soldiers, physicians, and statesmen. Apparently unembarrassed by this stupendous richness, the author of *Daughter of France* has plunged into the flood, extricated her heroine adroitly and without fuss, administered artificial respiration, wrung out her pseudo-classic draperies, thrown away the disguising weeds, and set her up as it were on the right bank of history, for all to see.

The reasons why V S-W chose to write this biography seem to have been quite different from those that led her to write the lives of Saint Joan and the two Teresas. In the case of the three saints her interest appears to have been fundamentally in their actions and in the reasons why they acted as they did, rather than in the personality of the women themselves, although the latter was naturally not ignored. In other words, it was the abstract religious aspects of their lives that she was mainly concerned with.

In *Daughter of France,* on the other hand, V S-W's interest seems to be far more in the personality, the character, and the background of La Grande Mademoiselle. Although V S-W explicitly states that *"Le*

Grand Siècle is not quite me somehow," she moves in it with as much ease and understanding as if she felt herself to be a direct descendant of the courtiers of Louis XIV. There are some aspects of Mademoiselle's character that V S-W seizes upon with especial interest, for example her love for and trust in her worthless father, Gaston, who is presented as being an amusing and affectionate father to her, at least during the years of her childhood. There were, in fact, quite a number of points in which there was a decided resemblance between the writer and her subject. Both came from an aristocratic background and were keenly conscious of the fact; both suffered from not having been born boys; both had a real love of castles and shared an interest in building and architecture: there was a great deal about Mademoiselle with which V S-W could identify herself. However, although V S-W makes much of those sides of her character and circumstances that she finds appealing, this does not mean that she was blind to her weaknesses. Far from it:

> It is primarily as a splendiferous figure of fun that she is depicted by her new biographer. True, Miss Victoria Sackville-West is warmly attached to her endearing heroine; but the portrait she has drawn is that of an over-excitable maiden aunt—"clumsy," "tactless" and "shallow-pated," bound to make a fool of herself, whether she dabbled in warfare and political intrigue or fell a victim to romantic passion.

Right from the beginning V S-W makes it quite clear that her clumsy, touching heroine is marked down for failure in life, in spite of all the advantages with which she was born. She does not attempt to excuse La Grande Mademoiselle, or to conceal the fact that she was in many respects a slightly ridiculous figure; "her clear-sighted criticisms, amounting sometimes to condemnation, are so cunningly infiltrated that the reader begins at last to take Mademoiselle's side against her [V S-W]." Nevertheless, the extent to which V S-W was in tune with Mademoiselle enabled her to present a picture of her that is both pathetic and endearing, and brings out to the full "the simple, touching grandeur of the unselfconscious and the sincere."

Even before *Daughter of France* appeared in print, V S-W had commenced work on her last novel, *No Signposts in the Sea*. Most of the book was written, appropriately enough, on board ship, for it was begun in January 1959, on the Nicolsons' annual cruise, that year to

Tokyo and Saigon, and the bulk of the writing was done on the cruise
in January and February 1960, to South Africa. Twice work on the
novel was interrupted by illness; V S-W suffered from severe attacks
of virus pneumonia for two months in the summer of 1959, and again
the following summer, with the result that the book was not finished
until the autumn of that year, and was not published until early 1961.

The *Times Literary Supplement* points out that the theme of the
book is one that V S-W has dealt with before:

> Years ago, in *All Passion Spent,* Miss Sackville-West wrote about an
> old lady waiting serenely and peacefully for death. Her new
> novel, . . . explores further the idea that acceptance of one's end
> obliterates self-pity and fear. It is in the form of a diary written
> during a Far-Eastern cruise by Edmund Carr, a middle-aged po-
> litical columnist who knows he will never return to the hurly-
> burly of power-struck society. He has chosen to spend his last
> weeks in the company of the one woman he has ever loved,
> though determined she shall never know his feelings or his fate.

This is perfectly correct. But the book also takes up two themes that
V S-W has dealt with in another novel, *The Dark Island:* they are
jealousy and the need for personal privacy. *No Signposts in the Sea* gives
a brilliant account of how Carr, who, near the beginning of the voyage
can say to Laura with unconscious irony, "I have never known the
meaning of jealousy," gradually becomes its victim to the extent that,
by jealousy and his own inferiority complex, he is totally blinded to
the fact that she is in love with him. He interprets her hints at the
truth as referring to the man he supposes to be his rival, the hated
Colonel Dalrymple. But masculine jealousy is not the only kind to be
examined in the book. During a conversation with Edmund Carr on
the subject of love and marriage, Laura says:

> "I knew two women, Lesbians, who lived for years together in a
> harmony more idyllic than the majority of marriages. . . . You
> look sceptical, but I assure you that it was love, deep, sincere,
> and in its way beautiful."
> "What was the snag, then?"
> "Jealousy. You say you don't know the meaning of the word.
> These two knew it, in all its cruellest refinements, especially the
> one who made a confidante of me; she was the more masculine of
> the two. You see, if a man is jealous of a woman, he at least meets

his rival on level ground, man to man; but if a woman is jealous of a woman, she enters into an unfair competition with the other sex; she is always afraid that the natural thing will conquer in the end. In this case the other woman, Lucy, the feminine one, was highly attractive to men, and though I don't believe she ever responded there was always the danger that she might some day do so. I can't tell you what torments my poor friend went through. She would seize upon every tiny circumstance and construe it according to her suspicions. She hated herself for it, for at heart she was really rather a noble creature, but that's the devil of jealousy: it transforms people. . . ."

It rings so true that one cannot help wondering if V S-W is not recalling emotions she herself experienced during her affair with Violet Trefusis in the 1920's.

As might be expected, the book is more than a record of Edmund Carr's reflections on his approaching death combined with a beautifully written love story. It appears also to be a summing up, ad-

Harold Nicolson and V. Sackville-West, 1955.

dressed to H.N., of V S-W's married life, the principles that have guided it, and the success that it has been. For her, the essentials of a successful marriage appear to be a certain reticence and the necessity for both man and wife to share the same sense of values. Speaking through Laura, V S-W adds:

> There is nothing more lovely in life than the union of two people whose love for one another has grown through the years from the small acorn of passion into a great rooted tree. Surviving all vicissitudes, and rich with its manifold branches, every leaf holding its own significance. . . . Such a love can be achieved only by the practice of mutual respect and personal liberty.

As an illustration of what she means, she quotes the following lines:

> Let there be spaces in your togetherness
> And let the winds of heaven dance between you.
>
> Sing and dance together and be joyous and let each one of
>   you be alone,
> Even as the strings of a lute are alone though they quiver
>   with the same music.
>
> Stand together, yet not too near together;
> For the pillars of the temple stand apart
> And the oak tree and the cypress grow not in each other's
>   shadow.

THIS ATMOSPHERE OF SUMMING UP together with the preoccupation with the nearness of death that permeate the whole story make it difficult not to believe that the book is a conscious leave-taking of this world in general, and H.N. in particular. There is no other evidence that V S-W was aware in 1960 of her approaching death. On the other hand, the fact that she tried to conceal from H.N. that she had a serious hemorrhage in January 1962 makes it doubtful whether she would have given any clearer indication of her knowledge than is contained in *No Signposts in the Sea,* even if she had been aware of how short a time remained.

In the book there is one passage in which there can be little doubt that V S-W is describing in symbolic terms the meaning of life as she

sees it, and the fact that death is an absolute end. It is where she gives
an account of the Man Overboard practice that is rehearsed on board
the ship one day in the tropics. A lighted canister of petrol has been
dropped into the ocean to simulate the man who is supposed to have
fallen overboard:

> Apparently they had no intention of trying to reach him; no life-
> boat was lowered; they contented themselves with watching the
> canister carried further and further away on some unseen cur-
> rent. It all seemed to me as unintelligible as many other things in
> life. One could hope only that it made sense to someone in au-
> thority. Meanwhile it was pitiable to see that small object strug-
> gling to survive, quaking and abandoned in an inexplicable
> waste; the flame dwindled once, and I thought it had been extin-
> guished, but it revived in the diminished flicker of a last determi-
> nation. Then it came to the edge of the lagoon, was buffeted by
> the ridge of our wake, tossed desperately for a moment, and was
> gone for ever.
> There are no tombstones in the sea.

The book contains yet another motif that is of importance in considering V S-W and her work. Just as Laura is presented as a touch-
stone by which standards of behavior in marriage are to be tested, so
Mervyn Dalrymple appears as a criterion to be used when judging
standards of general behavior. Again and again Edmund Carr, even
in the middle of his fits of jealousy, measures his thoughts and actions
by what the colonel would consider to be the right thing, for he cannot but admire him. "I wish that I could dislike the man I hate."

It is interesting to see what sort of person V S-W has chosen to
play this role. The virtues that are explicitly accorded to Colonel
Dalrymple by Carr, his rival, are many and varied. "He is genuine and
unself-conscious through and through; and so modest that if he had
the V.C., which perhaps he has, he would be at pains to conceal it."
Carr considers him "by no means stupid or ill-informed" and likes
"the out-of-the-way information which he imparts from time to time
without insistence . . . [he] has used his eyes and kept his ears open."
In several places it is made clear that although Dalrymple is intelligent
and well-informed, he never parades his knowledge or is too intelligent—he is not "clever" in the sense that an Englishman would
regard as being uncomplimentary. There is "a touch of rough poetry
about him" and he "can't stand the sight of a beast in distress." He is,

in fact, "so unmistakably English. Well-bred English." The ideal portrait that emerges is thus that of the "best type of English gentleman," and all that he stands for.

A love of England and Englishness is a very salient feature of V S-W's character. Partly, no doubt, this is because by birth and upbringing she was very conscious of belonging to the class of Englishman which for centuries has provided the material from which the history of England was woven. By blood, however, she did not belong wholly to this class, and an awareness of this may have made the need to identify herself with England stronger than it is in most people. There can be little doubt that in her father V S-W saw personified and idealized much of what she valued most in England and the English, for characters that bear a resemblance to him figure in many of her books. The greatest monument to her love and devotion to England is *The Land,* although this love runs through many of her works. The clearest expression of her ideal of the English gentleman is Colonel Dalrymple in *No Signposts in the Sea.*

THERE REMAINS LITTLE TO RELATE after the publication of her last novel in 1961. All that year V S-W enjoyed apparent good health, and was able to write a long short story, which was published in a magazine. In January 1962, however, she had a hemorrhage in the train on the way down to Southampton, where they were to embark for their cruise to the West Indies. She made no mention of this to H.N. Even in her diary she wrote no more than *"Disastrous* journey. I am very worried and confide in E. [Edith Lamont]."

On their return from the cruise, V S-W consulted a doctor. He advised an exploratory operation, which was undertaken on 1st March and revealed abdominal cancer. Although V S-W did make a partial recovery from the operation and was able to come downstairs again and see her garden in May, she complained that she seemed unable to get her strength back, and at the end of May she suffered a sudden relapse.

She died at Sissinghurst on 2nd June, 1962, and was buried a few days later in the Sackville crypt at Withyham.

CHAPTER VI

❦ Fiction ❦

V S-W DOES NOT SEEM to have been one of those people with an instinctive ability to seize instantly upon the vital point of an argument. Her son Nigel Nicolson says after mentioning that she had no desire to share the world of men, "nor had she the gift of logical reasoning." This is perhaps somewhat harsh. It might be more accurate to say that logical reasoning was a process that she had to learn to use, and that it was a considerable effort for her.

When confronted with some personal problem that affected her deeply, it seems unlikely that V S-W was able to discuss it and obtain relief in that manner. Her difficulty in establishing contact with other people was so great that she would hardly have been able to avail herself of this form of catharsis. Of all the people in the world, H.N. was probably the only one with whom she could discuss almost anything, but even with him there were obviously subjects that she could not bring herself, or did not wish, to mention. As she points out in *No Signposts in the Sea,* reticence is a virtue that she values highly in marriage. Clearly she did not normally discuss with him the book that she was working on at the moment, for she says herself, referring to when she was writing *No Signposts in the Sea,* "I thought how odd it was, you and I writing away in our little cabins, not knowing what the other was writing about, and then discovering it in print months later."

Instead of discussing her deepest problems, V S-W wrote about them in her novels. As she was aware, she was of a passionate disposition, the sort of person who would find it difficult to come to a true understanding of herself. But by transferring the problem to a fictional character in a fictional situation, she created for herself the possibility of placing sufficient distance between herself and the problem to enable her to regard it dispassionately and reach some logical conclusion. This appears to be what she did during her first period of fiction writing, from 1919 to 1924. These were the years when her mother had just left her father and was beginning to grow more and more eccentric, and also the years when she and H.N. lived through a serious crisis in their married life. The fiction she wrote then, *Heritage, The Dragon in Shallow Water, The Heir, Grey Wethers,* and *Challenge,* explores problems of heredity and duality, and an atmosphere of violence and revolt is noticeable in several, particularly in *The Dragon in Shallow Waters.*

Whether the inclusion in these early works of her deep-set fears and doubts was intentional or not there seems no way of telling, but it may well have been half-consciously done. Conscious or unconscious, there is beneath the surface of the majority of these works an undercurrent of unrest and self-searching. In *Seducers in Ecuador,* the last novel of the first period, even the most casual reader can hardly fail to be aware that this is a complex story which is certainly about a great deal more than a voyage in the Mediterranean and a murder trial.

V S-W wrote no fiction between 1924 and 1930. When she returned to it with *The Edwardians, All Passion Spent,* and *Family History,* it is a somewhat different kind of novel that we meet. Here there is little trace of introspection or of hidden depths; these are fairly open, straightforward stories. It is worth noting also that the first two are the novels that many critics consider her best; they are beyond question the most successful. *The Edwardians* became an immediate bestseller, and both this and *All Passion Spent* have gone through reprint after reprint, the latest being in 1970 and 1971 respectively, forty years after they were first published. The fourth novel of the second period, *The Dark Island,* strikes a different note. In this somber book, the last work of fiction V S-W was to write for eight years, she paints a scene which, like those in her early novels, gives a sense of dark emotions that are only partially revealed in the story.

With the exception of *Daughter of France* and two works which appear in part to have the character of exorcism, the remainder of V S-W's literary output is concerned, directly or indirectly, to a greater or lesser extent, with religious questions—aspects of divine revelation; the existence of God; life after death. As regards her remaining fiction, *Grand Canyon, The Easter Party,* and *No Signposts in the*

Sea, a change seems to come over her writing. The difference that gradually becomes apparent may be described as the emergence in the novel of a thesis, or inner story, which is sometimes very different from the plot.

It seems quite probable that it is the parallel existence of thesis and plot that L. A. G. Strong, writing in the *Spectator,* is referring to when, in a review of *The Easter Party,* he points out:

> Every novel written by a poet is in one sense an allegory. If it moves him as a poet—and he has no business with it otherwise—its characters and scenes will bear more than their literal meaning. Like a poem, it will contain more than the poet is consciously aware of as he writes it. Miss Sackville-West's work has always had this double validity. Even where she is least conscious of her intentions, the truth of her work rings on more than one level.

Strong evidently takes the view that V S-W was probably not aware of the fact that the novels she wrote were capable of being interpreted at different levels. He may be right, and it would certainly be difficult to refute his opinion categorically. There are nevertheless small indications that, as far as the thesis contained in some of her novels is concerned, V S-W might have been conscious of the fact that they do contain more than appears on the surface, that they can be interpreted in more ways than one, and that she might even have intended this to be so.

One of the main reasons for suspecting that a thesis has not crept into V S-W's books without her knowledge is that it sometimes appears to be so carefully concealed.Whereas one can hardly come to the end of *Heritage* without realizing that the author is keenly interested in problems arising out of mixed heredity, it is easy to close *The Easter Party* without realizing that, beneath the surface, this is a book whose essential concern is with religious problems. This is probably because the clues to the inner story, the thesis, are scattered throughout the book concealed in unobtrusive little pieces of information, incidents, comments, fragments of dialogue, and other indications which, if carefully collected and pieced together, give a different view of what the book is about than that given by the main story. Seen in this way, Sir Walter Mortibois, Q.C., emerges as an austere man dedicated with monklike celibacy to the quest for a religious ideal according to which he can live.

In *No Signposts in the Sea,* V S-W uses the same technique as in *The*

Easter Party. The phrase which gives the book its name precedes and acts as a pointer to the more significant phrase "there are no tombstones in the sea." Furthermore, the "man overboard practice" and Edmund Carr's burial at sea bear too great a likeness to each other in description and significance for it to be accidental.

The inclusion of a thesis in V S-W's work appears to date from *Solitude* (1938). This poem, the whole tone of which is clearly religious, does not yield up its personal meaning until certain lines and passages are picked out and pieced together. In this poem, these seem to be included in an arbitrary order which is not always the order in which they should logically be arranged; it is, however, not difficult to pick them out or to rearrange them. Both the poem itself and the personal reflections are religious in nature, and they blend into a harmonious whole.

In *The Garden,* on the other hand, the thesis, once again religious, is not only quite different from the motif of the poem itself, but is also far better hidden. It is quite possible to read and appreciate *The Garden* without paying any regard to the thesis. If both are considered together, however, they will be found to harmonize well despite their apparent dissimilarity.

In between these two poems comes the novel *Grand Canyon.* The failure of this strange book is quite possibly due to V S-W's inability in this, her first attempt in a prose work, to fuse together thesis and plot. It is clear that this must be a much more difficult thing to do in a novel, which must have a plot, than in a poem, which need not. Although she succeeded much better in *The Easter Party,* it was not until she wrote *No Signposts in the Sea* that a fusion of the two was successfully accomplished. This she achieved by reducing plot to a minimum, a mere framework for her ideas.

V S-W can hardly be described as a popular novelist in the sense that her works were written with an eye to the reaction of her public. Two of her novels, however, *The Edwardians* and *All Passion Spent,* can be described as popular in the sense that they caught and retained general attention. In the majority of her books she seems rather to have written to satisfy personal needs.

It may seem strange that an author whose work is frequently of so personal an origin can allow her books to be published. A statement V S-W once made during an interview goes far toward explaining this. She could never, she said, discuss her work with others when she was writing it. "I can't even mention it, or it gets tarnished. It's an intensely private matter. The minute it's gone to the publisher it's gone from you, and means nothing more to you."

THE QUALITY MOST IMMEDIATELY apparent in V S-W's work is the beauty of her prose, an observation which applies equally to her fiction, her biographies, and her travel books. It is, however, a style that she had to discipline herself to achieve; restraint was not a trait that came naturally to her passionate nature. The tranquillity and balance which are such noticeable features of *No Signposts in the Sea,* her last novel, are by no means equally obvious in *Heritage,* her first. In her early fiction, the extent to which V S-W was able to master style seems to be related in part to the strength of the emotions that the characters in her books arouse in her and the degree to which she had learnt to subjugate these emotions; it is illuminating to note that the first work in which balance and harmony of style are achieved is the beautifully written short story "The Heir" (1922), in which the chief character is not really a person at all, but an ancient English manor house. With growing command over her emotions and greater experience she is able to handle a story as full of potential dangers as *The Dark Island* with complete mastery. It is, however, a precarious mastery, for when she wrote *Grand Canyon* eight years later, neither style nor story are equal in quality to those of the immediately preceding works, possibly because she was writing in time of war on a subject about which she felt strongly and instinctively rather than analyzed with her intellect.

V S-W's prose style is the perfect vehicle for conveying atmosphere, which, in much of her fiction has an important function to fulfil. Based on an acute power of observation and a poet's gift of expressing in emotive language what has been observed, atmosphere is always vividly communicated, and experienced as an integral part of the story. Very often atmosphere is connected with a place or the surrounding countryside, as with the Elizabethan house in *The Heir,* the Downs and the sarsen stones in *Grey Wethers,* the Greek archipelago in *Challenge,* Storn in *The Dark Island,* and, to a lesser extent, with the Fens and the factory in *The Dragon in Shallow Waters,* Anstey in *The Easter Party,* and with the Grand Canyon. In all these books the atmosphere V S-W creates around a place influences the thoughts and actions of some or all of the characters in a manner over which they seem to have little control. In other books, notably *All Passion Spent* and *No Signposts in the Sea,* the whole story is permeated with a gentle but unmistakable note of melancholy, providing a shimmer of pathos and dignity.

V S-W's fiction contains many memorable characters; the finest of them are usually women. As with style, however, portrayal of character is an art which she has had to learn, and it has demanded self-discipline and training. The inability fully to control her own emotions is, however, not the only reason why some characters, particularly in the early novels, fail to become completely believable people, although it undoubtedly bears some of the blame. Like Jane Austen, V S-W is an author who is truly at home only with a narrow cross-section of society: the upper middle class whose wealth is derived, not from trade, but from land or some profession. If she remains within these limits, she is able to create such finely observed characters as Lady Slane in *All Passion Spent* and Laura Drysdale in *No Signposts in the Sea.* This also applies to Shirin le Breton, née Wilson, in *The Dark Island,* who, although lower middle class by birth, is very definitely not so by temperament or inclination. Unlike Jane Austen, however, V S-W sometimes ventures outside this field to portray people from other classes, and the result is not always equally felicitous. Not that these characters lack force; Silas and Gregory Dene in *The Dragon in Shallow Waters* are vigorously, even violently, drawn, but they never become convincing in the same way as, for example, Lady Slane does. This is true of dialogue, too. V S-W is not at her best with people such as the Denes, whose idiom is clearly not her own. The sure touch and the awareness of subtle or unspoken nuances which is typical of *The Dark Island* and other books if often lacking, with the inevitable result that the credibility of the characters is weakened. She probably realized this weakness herself rather early, for in the collection of short stories she published in 1922, *The Heir,* interior monologue has replaced much of the dialogue; indeed, the servant girl who is the main character of "The Parrot," the last story in the book, makes only one direct utterance, and that is a quotation from the 160th Hymn. At the other end of the scale, her portrayal of the aristocracy in *The Edwardians* also lacks the depth and rotundity which would have made the characters in the book come truly alive, but this, surely, is partly intentional—the emptiness of the aristocratic characters is heavily stressed—and partly because they are caricatures, at least to some extent.

In other novels the flatness of the characters is clearly intentional:

Lomax, Bellamy, and Miss Whitaker in *Seducers in Ecuador,* for instance, make no pretence to reality. They are mere pawns of fate, and
to have made them living personalities set against a vivid background
would have entirely robbed the story of its point. *Grand Canyon* is a
similar case. It is not a realistic story; neither are the characters drawn
in a realistic manner. In this connection it is worth noting that V S-W
sometimes gave her characters names such as Clare, Bellamy, Temple, Mortibois, which invite an allegorical interpretation.

The originality of V S-W's fiction was early noticed by several critics, first, perhaps, by Amy Lowell in a very long review of *The Dragon
in Shallow Waters* in the *New York Times.* Lowell complains that "I had
gradually been realizing that I could not read a novel through. People
who I trusted would recommend this or that one to me. I would rush
out and buy it, only to find my interest wither before I had got a
quarter way through. Many of them were excellently done, but, alas, I
know their types so fatiguingly well! Their developments and cli-
maxes are as familiar as the multiplication table, and I am no more
thrilled by their conclusions than I am by the fact that twelve times
twelve is a hundred and forty-four." But, she goes on to say, "the
other day I had a sensation—I came across a novel which I actually
read from the first page to the last; what is more, after a lapse of several months I read it again, and it held me the second time." Amy
Lowell does not acclaim the novel a masterpiece; she admits its faults,
but praises it for its atmosphere, its insight into human nature, and,
above all, for its freshness and originality—those qualities that are to
be found in many of V S-W's short stories and novels, in the daring
challenge to the reader at the very end of *Devil at Westease* (1947), for
example.

Plot is an aspect of V S-W's fiction not of the same importance in
her writing as it is in that of many other authors. Only one of her
books, *Devil at Westease,* has a plot that could possibly be described as
complicated, and only here is it essential that this should be so, for
upon the fact that the reader is kept in the dark as to the true identity
of the murderer depends the whole effectiveness of the story. Development of character in V S-W's novels is, on the whole, less the result
of events and the unfolding of a plot than of inheritance, the irony of
fate, the interaction of personalities, or the power of nature or a place
to mould a person's being. To this extent she is a Naturalist. The best
of her fiction, however, is almost invariably that with the slightest plot:
the short stories, *All Passion Spent, No Signposts in the Sea.* This is also

the reason why the short story and the short novel proved to be such very suitable forms for her fiction.

V S-W is a difficult writer of fiction to evaluate. Like other good novelists, her development is marked by maturing style, increasing technical skill, and an awareness of her own limitations. But she differs from them in several respects. She is a poet before she is a novelist, and her gift of observation and vivid expression make it easier for her to master mood and atmosphere, which are always magnificently handled, than dialogue and character. Her concern with heredity and religious problems together with her difficulty in establishing contact with people sometimes result in the impression that she is writing more for herself than for her readers. Her passionate temperament creates many problems before she learns how to control it. But it is above all her originality and the very personal quality of much of her writing which make judgment difficult. In her review of *The Dragon in Shallow Waters,* Amy Lowell, speaking of reviews she has read, remarks: "no set of rules known to the reviewer could gauge it, so it was dismissed in a curt paragraph or two. Now, no one can quarrel with such treatment; when one perpetrates a satire and infuses it with tenderness and sympathy, what can one expect but to be misunderstood."

There is, as we have seen, a very personal quality about V S-W's fiction. Connected with this is the fact that she was very little influenced by other writers. *Grey Wethers* has similarities with *Wuthering Heights,* it is true, and *Seducers in Ecuador* reminds one a little of James, but apart from these early works, it is not easy to identify the influence of other authors. Even the great friendship with Virginia Woolf left remarkably little impression on V S-W's writing, as an American researcher has recently confirmed. This personal quality, together with her originality, are what distinguish V S-W from other writers.

CHAPTER VII

❦ Biographical Works ❦

THERE ARE PROBABLY only two ways of writing a successful modern biography: one employs an analytical, the other an intuitive approach. The difference between the two methods is not always so great as might be expected, nor is the intuitive approach necessarily the inferior one, as is sometimes assumed, even by people who ought to know better. Both methods are primarily dependent on the facts concerning the subject of the biography, facts which vary in authenticity from well-documented, incontrovertible certainty to ill-substantiated references of an ancedotal nature. To these must be added the subject's own writings and correspondence, the opinions of contemporaries, and the judgment of subsequent writers. When all this material has been sifted and evaluated, a task common to all biography, there remains the question of interpretation, and it is here that the subject must be fortunate in his choice of a biographer, for, despite the insight given by psychology into the causes of human behavior, to what extent does one person truly comprehend the actions and feelings of another unless there exists between them a bond of sympathy and understanding? The mere fact that a writer chooses his subject is some guarantee that there is, indeed, an attraction between them, for who would elect to write about a person for whom he does not feel a certain affinity or fascination? Moreover, biography being an art which is dependent upon selection, the selection made by the biographer must inevitably be influenced by his own scale of values. This means that all biography will be subjective, but as H.N. wrote in *The Development of English Biography,* "to a certain extent a subjective attitude is desirable and inevitable; and indeed the most perfect of English biographies, such as Lockhart's *Life of Scott,* inevitably contain or convey a sketch of the biographer subsidiary to that of the main portrait." Virginia Woolf went even further. In 1926 she wrote in a letter to V S-W: "Do we then know anybody? Only our own versions of them, which, as likely as not, are emanations from ourselves." It may probably be assumed that no biographer has ever consciously included in his work emanations from himself; they may nevertheless have crept in without his being aware of it. The very facts he selects, and his interpretation of them, may reveal more of himself than he intends, and the greater the extent to which he identifies with his subject, the more likely this is to happen.

In previous chapters we have seen some of the probable reasons why V S-W chose the six women and one man who were the subjects of her longer biographical works. These reasons were personal: either she was interested in some aspect of their writing, or she turned to them because she seems to have felt that something about their problems might be relevant to hers. It might be illuminating to look a little closer at her major biographies, and also at the article on George Eliot which she contributed to a collection of essays.

If we ignore the long preface to *The Diary of Lady Anne Clifford* (1923), V S-W's first essay in biography was *Aphra Behn: The Incomparable Astrea* (1927). In this book her primary concern was to rehabilitate "the first woman in England to earn her living by her pen," whose reputation had been severely damaged fourteen years earlier by Dr. Bernbaum. It is interesting to see how vigorously V S-W takes up the cudgels on behalf of Mrs. Behn, who "claimed equal rights with men; she was a phenomenon never before seen, and, when seen, furiously resented," particularly when one realizes that the years around 1927 saw the height of her friendship with Virginia Woolf, whose ideas on feminine rights may have influenced her. Interesting, too, is the attention paid to the mystery of Aphra Behn's birth, the possibility that her mother disapproved of her daughter scribbling verses, her inability to handle money, and the fact that she prized freedom in love so highly. It is, however, even more interesting to see how severely V S-W criticizes her heroine for her writing. She dismisses the novels, which, adopting the French, Spanish, or Italian convention, "then descend to an intolerable artificiality, and are readable only thanks to their brevity and to the colloquial raciness which was never absent from her style. The brevity of these novels is much to be thankful for." The playwright also receives short shrift: "And as she squandered her chances as a novelist,—neglecting to become, as she might have become, an invaluable *genre* painter,—as a playwright, though she did a trifle better, the improvement is so small that it serves only to fill us again with regret." And as for Astrea's claim that she was a poet, V S-W gives two examples from "the swell of her turgid Pindarics" and comments: "Is that poetry? . . . It is very seldom that her voice speaks with even this hint of the accent of poetry." Only for the novel *Oroonoko* and for the songs has V S-W any praise. The former is "the most original contribution made by her to English literature, . . . but even in that story, drawn out of her own life, she allowed her readings of the heroic romances to colour her description of colonial existence and to flavour her interpretation of her hero with an air of classic chivalry." "The songs are, on the whole, the best that can be claimed for her, and it may be said that the claim is a modest one."

Nothing in the biographical part of the book prepares the reader for the withering criticism of the final, evaluative section. It is as though V S-W takes Astrea's failure to be a better, more modern writer than her contemporaries almost as a personal affront. Could it be because she has, to some little extent, identified with Mrs. Behn, and feels the disappointment at finding her feet are made of clay more keenly on that account? She is, at any rate, aware of the unjustness of her criticism, for she adds: "Indeed, this whole estimate of Astrea's work is perhaps slightly ungracious: it is more in the nature of reproach than praise. We concede that she did certain things well, and then immediately attack her for not having done different things better." But the attack is nevertheless made.

WHEN V S-W WROTE HER MONOGRAPH on Andrew Marvell in 1929, she was venturing forth on to what was almost virgin territory. In his lifetime Marvell was well-known as a political satirist and, for over a hundred years after his death, he was also highly regarded as an incorruptible patriot. However, his lyrical and non-political poems, which contain his finest work, not only remained unpublished until three years after his death; they do not even seem to have been circulated in manuscript, as were the poems of the majority of his contemporaries. When they did finally appear in 1681, published by his housekeeper, Mary Palmer, calling herself Mary Marvell, they aroused no literary debate. During the following two hundred years we find, in England, occasional references to these lyrics: Wordsworth mentioned them to Walter Scott, Charles Lamb introduced them to Hazlitt and Leigh Hunt, a few were included in Campbell's *Specimens* (1819) and Hall's *Book of Gems* (1836), and Craik has something to say about Marvell in his *Sketches of the History of Literature* (1845), but it was not until Tennyson insisted that Palgrave include "An Horatian Ode" in *The Golden Treasury* (1861) that Marvell reached a wider public. Writers in America had been more perceptive: Emerson speaks of Marvell with admiration, Poe made an acute analysis of one of the poems included in the *Book of Gems,* and, in 1857, a volume of Marvell's *Poetical Works* was published in Boston, the first to show an interest in him as a poet. It was not until after the First World War, however, that any real criticism was devoted to him, the occasion then being the tercentenary of his birth in 1621, the critic, T. S. Eliot in his essay on the Metaphysical Poets.

When V S-W's book appeared eight years later, Marvell's poetry had not yet been bedeviled by what must surely be the most obscure, over-erudite, and misleading body of criticism that it has ever been the misfortune of a poet to incur, and she was consequently free to develop her own views, unhampered by previous opinions. For her, as we have seen, Marvell was a poet open to direct inspiration from nature, with which he experienced a communion described as "that sense of man's eventual harmony with nature, which for want of a better word we must call mysticism in this connection." She illustrated what she means with several quotations from the poems. Few of Marvell's subsequent critics would have agreed with V S-W on this point. Her case for Marvell as a poet whose inspiration came strongest from nature is strengthened, she feels, by the fact that he substituted for the traditional shepherd of bucolic poetry the mower of grass, the scythesman (who, in passing, figures prominently in her own poem *The Land*), thereby demonstrating that he regards nature as more than a mere convention. This pastoral poet, and the retiring man who loved privacy, are the gentle aspects of Marvell, for "his was a dual nature, and the gentler side went undermost." Conceits were an ornament, or a disfigurement, rather than an integral part of his poetry and occur most frequently in his non-bucolic poems. But they were, together with an energetic and virile public life, the other side of his nature, and eventually they drowned the voice of the poet.

In the light of modern scholarship, self-contradictory though much of it is, it seems very doubtful whether V S-W's interpretation of Marvell's poetic talent is sufficiently nuanced to be adequate; conceits, for instance, certainly played a more important part in his poems than she would allow. It does explain, however, why the two extracts from Marvell included in *Another World Than This,* the commonplace book edited by V S-W and H.N., are not particularly representative of the Marvell that most people recognize. V S-W's is a poet's view—indeed, the book is one of the series entitled "The Poets on the Poets"—and, as such, is both interesting and illuminating, not least for the light it casts on V S-W herself, on whose characteristics some of her estimates of Marvell are clearly founded.

THE ESSAY ON GEORGE ELIOT that V S-W published in 1932 is, quite predictably, concerned less with the novels, several of which are not even mentioned, than with the person, with the Mary Ann Evans who first defied her parents on a question of religion, then, in direct contravention of Victorian morals, eloped with a married man with whom she lived for the rest of her life, and, finally, with the woman who became a novelist at the age of thirty-seven. She does not go into the reasons why Mary Ann Evans wrote under the name of George Eliot, but she does "wonder what her feelings were, when for the first time she signed that name at the foot of a letter."

It is the contradictions in Mary Ann Evans that interest V S-W. Firstly, there is the discrepancy between her appearance and her temperament. "Without going so far as to suggest that anything resembling a dual personality existed in George Eliot, it is certain that her inner life and her consequent actions were by no means entirely in accordance with the large placidity of those familiar features. As we contemplate those features, it is hard to believe that she could ever be described as 'wayward and hysterical.' Yet such is the fact." Secondly, the fact that she who acted rebellion in her life did not preach it in her novels. "She was no flaming rebel, with a desire to scandalize and startle her generation. No dreams that her example might speed up the emancipation of her sex ever entered her head. Rather, she disapproved avowedly of the 'unsexing' of women, which was beginning to be talked about as she grew older." Thirdly, there is the contrast between Eliot the realist and Eliot the romantic. "Unfortunately . . . George Eliot the realist had her romantic side; few realists are without it; in George Eliot it took the form of creating impossibly romantic scamps or prigs of men, and of writing *Romola.*"

Renaissance Florence provided George Eliot with an opportunity, the only one she took, of escaping from her otherwise orderly intellectual existence, and she made the most of it. "She let herself go, and go badly, over Tito, less badly, over Tessa, who at any rate may claim relationship with Hetty Sorrel in *Adam Bede* (George Eliot had a persistent weakness for kittenish women). Then the whole background of fifteenth-century Florence provided her with an orgy of romantic indulgence: young men in scarlet tights, *barrette, zazzere,* and *scarselle*—cod pieces, too, though she averted her pen from those, if not her eyes." V S-W states quite clearly that George Eliot must not be judged by *Romola,* however interesting the novel may be as an indication of her several repressions. It is, however, the only book by Eliot that she discusses at any length.

AMONG THE MANY PORTRAITS in *Saint Joan of Arc* there are two of particular interest. One is, of course, Jeanne d'Arc herself; the other is the Dauphin, later Charles VII. They are presented as two strongly contrasting figures.

Jeanne d'Arc remains always the central figure in the book. Of her appearance, V S-W says: "We may presume her to have been a strong, healthy, plain and sturdy girl," adding, "I think it is not unfair to qualify her as unattractive . . . for all the excitement of her startling notoriety, she clearly aroused neither the natural desires of man nor the competitive distrust of women." As a child, she is described as probably "a serious and aloof little girl, even to the extent of being regarded as rather a prig by the other children." When she left Domremy to accomplish the double task of raising the siege of Orleans and leading a reluctant Dauphin to his coronation at Reims, the qualities in her that V S-W stresses most are her peasant shrewdness, common sense, and a sense of proportion. To these qualities she attributes her military successes, and also uses them to explain some of the phenomena that have by other people been described as miraculous. But she also shows a Jeanne capable of acting and speaking in so high-handed a manner that it would have been arrogant if V S-W had not clearly indicated that it was an expression of Jeanne's absolute certainty that her mission came from God himself. This Jeanne rebukes prelates and princes of the blood, castigates generals, and does not shrink from "browbeating a king into doing the bidding of the King of Kings." There was also, however, a softer side to her nature; her womanly voice and her ready tears. "She was, in fact, emotional, and wept copiously at every opportunity—as queer a mixture of feminine and masculine attributes as ever relentlessly assaulted the enemy and then must cry on seeing him hurt." Considerable stress is laid throughout the book on Jeanne's insistence on wearing male apparel, but this was, of course, one of the points which figured prominently during the trial. It is, however, given added emphasis here by the fact that V S-W introduces several comments on Jeanne's male attire during the account of her journey from Domremy to Chinon, her campaigns, and the events leading up to her capture and trial. One cannot help being reminded of V S-W's own exploits as "Julian" in Paris in 1918.

The Dauphin, on the other hand, is the antithesis of Jeanne d'Arc in almost every respect. He is described as having a miserable physique, with limbs so frail and weak that it gave people a shock to see him without his ennobling robe. His character was on a par with his appearance, but this, in V S-W's view, was partly the result of his bad heredity. Charles VI suffered from periods of insanity, but there seems to be some doubt whether he was the Dauphin's true father. More interesting is what V S-W has to say about his mother, Isabeau de Bavière. She "was a woman of the dominating type which tends to produce weak sons. . . . The pressure of her personality on him in his early years must have been crushing, and, moreover, it was his misfortune to be born with a nature meekly resigned to accept insults."

The differences between these two people are brought out in many places: where the Dauphin was weak and vacillating, Jeanne was strong and single-minded; where he was prepared to betray her, she was faithful to him; where he apparently never felt any sense of duty toward France, she never deviated from her allegiance to Heaven. V S-W sums it up by saying of him: "as Charles VII of France, his character emerges with so little honour from his association with Jeanne d'Arc that one can scarcely restrain a smile of amusement at the ironical contrast between such protagonists as the weak, knock-kneed, pious little man and the avenging virgin descending on him from the confines of his kingdom, bent not only on forcing him to do all kinds of things he had no inclination whatsoever to do, but convinced, in a way which allowed of no open contradiction, of his ardent, if latent, willingness to do them."

PEPITA (1937) IS A biography that has, of necessity, been discussed at some length in previous chapters of this study, where it has been related to the events of V S-W's life. It is therefore necessary to add only one comment here. In the excellent and illuminating book about his parents Nigel Nicolson recently published, *Portrait of a Marriage,* he writes that, in *Pepita,* V S-W "drew portraits of her parents that do too much honour to her father and too little to her mother," who was, in fact, "a woman of strong will softened by charm and oversweetened by sentimentality." There is probably some truth in this, particularly as regards her father, whom she obviously idolized. Her mother, on the other hand, despite her great charm, seems at times to have been a formidable woman whose increasing eccentricity and difficultness are well documented in H.N.'s *Diaries and Letters.* It is quite possible that Lady Sackville was less indulgent to her daughter than to a grandson who was born when she was fifty-five years old.

IF V S-W HAD WANTED to identify with St. Teresa of Avila, there is a good deal in the story of her life as told in *The Eagle and the Dove* that would have made it easy for her to do so, particularly in those parts of the book that are concerned with her background and youth. She was of aristocratic birth, coming from a family in Old Castile, where, as V S-W points out, the people are noted for extreme racial pride and arrogance. As a child, Teresa was not only something of a tomboy, but also had a vivid imagination, which she apparently fed by reading a large number of romances, with the result that she and her brother Rodrigo one day decided to run away from home in order to seek martyrdom in Africa. Like V S-W, however, they were soon discovered and brought back again. At sixteen, she entered the Dominican convent of Santa Maria de Gracia, not because she felt she had a vocation, but because she was sent there by her father, who had apparently discovered a lesbian relationship between Teresa, her cousin, and a third girl. For the mature Teresa, V S-W has nothing but respect and admiration. Her indomitable will and courage, her capability, her good-humored practical common-sense, her intellectual ability, and her religious gifts figure prominently in the biography. This combination of practical talents and mystical vision is evidently one that interests V S-W a great deal, for, when explaining why Teresa set out on journeys that took her through much of Spain, always in discomfort and often ill and in pain, in order to found new Carmelite houses, she gives as a reason: "the duality of her nature, half active, half contemplative, came to disturb any settled existence,

and after thirty-four years of convent life she took to the road, never
again to leave it."

Saint Thérèse of Lisieux does indeed provide the contrast fore-
shadowed in the subtitle. Against the almost masculine intellect of the
Spanish saint is set the purely feminine intelligence of the French girl:
"the Velasquez or the El Greco opposed to the oleograph. Not ac-
cidentally have they been accorded the epithets of 'the great' and 'the
little.' The Spaniard enjoyed the double aristocracy of birth and intellect, the French girl belonged by birth to the bourgeoisie and intellectually to the direct and simple."

It is clear that V S-W is both attracted to and repelled by St.
Thérèse. She devotes a long section of the book to her youth and her
early awareness "that I was born for glory, and searching for the
means to attain it, it was inwardly revealed to me that my own glory
would never appear to mortal eyes, but would consist in becoming a
saint. This desire might seem full of temerity, but I still feel the same
audacious confidence that I shall become a *great saint*." "In secular
life," comments V S-W, "a parallel self-confidence might incur a
charge of arrogance." Her admiration for the pertinacity with which
Thérèse sought admission to Carmel, despite repeated rebuffs, is unmistakable, but so is her ambivalence regarding the Little Way that
is the saint's contribution to the Catholic faith. The subjugation of an
often unruly spirit that was necessary in order to create and follow the
Little Way was a supreme achievement. "Never to fail in the smallest
particular; never the slightest relaxation of vigilance; the minutest
slip on the self-imposed path to be instantly corrected and the balance restored; to act not dutifully but joyfully; to train the character
by incessant practice until the eclipse of self became second nature;
it sounds obvious. Let any scoffer try the experiment conscientiously
even for a week, even for a day, and find that the Little Way is neither
so obvious nor so easy as it sounds." On the other hand, about the
book in which Thérèse described the Little Way she says: "It must be
admitted that much of *l'Histoire d'une âme* is intolerable to a different
kind of mind. The infantilism of Thérèse, the treacly dulcification,
the reduction of the difficult to the easy, which inspire so enthusiastic
a devotion and response in some, provoke an equal exasperation in
others. . . . There is, to some minds, something infuriating about
the imagery and phraseology we encounter, as nauseating as a sur-
feit of marshmallows. The untranslatable words *mièvrerie* and even
niaiserie, words which one of her most devoted admirers among her

own countrymen has not hesitated to apply, can in English be rendered only by such adjectives as sugary, namby-pamby, and silly." V S-W restores the balance by concluding: "It would be but a shallow spirit, however, which peered exclusively and with dismissive irritation at Thérèse's mannerisms, for the tough core of heroism is there, even if it must be disinterred from under layers and layers of cotton-wool."

If we have dwelt on the differences between the masculine Teresa and the feminine Thérèse and the emphasis given to these differences in *The Eagle and the Dove,* we must not ignore the essential feature that these two saints had in common; that both were mystics, for it was of great importance to V S-W. As we have already seen, she considered that there was a greater resemblance between the creative artist and the mystic than between any other brands of human beings. However, it was probably not merely with the similarity between inspiration and vision that she was concerned, but also with the failure of inspiration and vision: St. John of the Cross's *Dark Night of the Soul;* her own "horrible loneliness of the soul." Was there not some message of hope to be found in the lives of the saints?

La Grande Mademoiselle, Anne Marie Louise d'Orléans, duchesse de Montpensier in her own right, first cousin to King Louis XIV of France, le roi soleil, differs in one important respect from the subjects of all V S-W's other biographies. She excelled in nothing. On the contrary, "there was a touch of the clown about Mademoiselle, something unwise and ill-advised, something rash and silly, something half-comic, half-heroic, something which endeared her to a populace always more prompt to acclaim a figure they could laugh at than a figure they must solemnly admire." The difference is reflected in V S-W's attitude to her subject.

Mademoiselle was born in 1627, daughter to the richest heiress in France, Marie de Bourbon, and Gaston, duc d'Orléans, the spineless brother of Louis XIII. She grew up to be a large, rather plain, masculine woman related to, or acquainted with, nearly all the people who moulded the history of the mid-seventeenth century. She played a prominent part in that tragi-comic civil war known as the Fronde, "capturing" Orleans without a shot during the Fronde of the Princes in 1652, and later causing the cannon of the Bastille to be fired on the royal armies under the command of Marshal Turenne, for which she was banished from Paris for five years. In 1670, when she was forty-three years old, Mademoiselle, who had refused to consider marriage with any of the princes of Europe, including the future Charles II of England, fell suddenly and violently in love with Antonin Nompar de Caumont, marquis de Puyguilhem, usually known as M. de Lauzun. This arrogant, ambitious, tiny little man, who had raised himself from nothing to a position of great trust at court and had become one of Louis XIV's favorites, treated her with a mixture of sympathy and offhandedness, now hot, now cold, which merely served to increase her infatuation, without, it seems, having any real intention of marrying her. Finally, however, she cornered him and, in December 1690, even persuaded the King to give his sanction to their wedding. Four days later, on the eve of the ceremony, Louis was compelled by the weight of public opinion to rescind his approval of this *mésalliance;* they were to be allowed to go on meeting, but there could no longer be any question of their marrying. Mademoiselle was brokenhearted, but worse was to follow. Almost exactly a year later M. de Lauzun was suddenly arrested and thrown into prison in the distant fortress of Pignerol. For the next ten years Mademoiselle did everything in her power to obtain his release, but without success until she agreed to hand over a considerable portion of her fortune to the duc du Maine, the son of the King's mistress, Mme. de Montespan, against her promise to intercede with the King. Lauzun obtained his release, but repaid Mademoiselle for all her trouble by insulting her repeatedly, carrying on with other women, and extorting from her money which he spent on gambling and on other amusements until, in the end, she could stand it no longer, and told him to take himself off. She died, aged sixty-six, in 1693, but even after her death Fate could still play her a cruel trick: "She lay in state, her body invigilated for several days, two hours at a time, by a duchess or a princess and by two ladies of quality. . . . A most ridiculous thing then happened. In mid-ceremony, the urn containing the entrails exploded with a frightful noise and an insufferable stink. Instantly, some of the ladies were swooning with horror, others taking flight. The heralds, and the monks of St. Bernard in the act of singing psalms, all made for the doors, together with the crowd who pushed even harder than they did. The chaos was extreme."

It is not difficult to see what attracted V S-W to la Grande Mademoiselle, for in several respects they had a great deal in common. "She had not been born with a masculine mind, which is, perhaps, the deepest failure of her life, if she had only known it. Had she been

born a thoroughly feminine woman she could have found her fulfilment in a dozen natural ways, but Nature had endowed her with
many of the attributes usually ascribed to the male, as her contemporaries were not slow to recognize. . . . Rough and forthright, honest
and spacious, her nature in many ways matched her physique. She
must have appeared very large and hoydenish in a Court peopled by
soft, perfidious, intriguing and amorous women." She developed a
great interest in houses and gardens, taking personal charge of the
rebuilding of the chateaux of St. Fargeau and Eu, and also the design-
ing of her new house at Choisy, just outside Paris. She was very conscious of her birth; frank and always true to herself; quick to recognize her own failings; no believer in docile submission to men; she was
generous, never doing anything by halves; and she never liked being
the center of attention—all characteristics which V S-W was well
acquainted with. It is possible that Mademoiselle's tragic love for
Lauzun may have reminded her of her own passionate affairs, and,
though this must remain a conjecture, it is also a possibility that the
streak of cruelty which undoubtedly existed within her, rejoiced a
little at the humiliation of Mademoiselle.

V S-W never makes any attempt to conceal Mademoiselle's failings; rather the reverse. She stresses the fact that she was a goose, but
does so with a tenderness and affection that make the biography a
warm and moving study. The fact that Mademoiselle excelled in
nothing, her very weaknesses, give V S-W a comfortable sense of pro-
tective superiority, absent in her other biographies, toward her
clumsy heroine, at the same time as her affinity with Mademoiselle
allows her real insight into her character. This keen sense of partici-
pation, which is the source of the many strengths of the book, is
perhaps also responsible for the weak moment: discussing the complicated state of Mademoiselle's finances after the death of her father,
V S-W bursts out into an irritated reflection which several critics have
commented upon. It is a minor point, perhaps the only complaint that
can be made against a biography notable not only for the very living
portrait of its subject, but also for the sureness with which she creates
both the large canvas of events in France and the smaller one of ev-
eryday life in the seventeenth century.

IT SEEMS THAT there are indeed emanations from V S-W in her
biographies. It is perhaps not altogether surprising that this should be

so, for as we have already seen, she frequently uses her own experiences and projects aspects of her own personality and problems into her novels and poetry. This raises the question of whether a biography containing such obvious emanations can be regarded as satisfactory, as giving a true portrait of the subject as he really was. Is it not bound to be a falsification to some extent, to be twisted out of shape by the bias of the biographer? Not necessarily. It must be remembered that we are dealing here with a question of selection and interpretation only—the facts always remain the same. If the biographer and his subject happen to have a great deal in common, particularly as regards background and personality, he will probably be able accurately to interpret his subject's reactions by observing his own. Emanations are a form of identification. If the identification is correct, and the biographer and his subject really do share a number of common features, it seems likely that the *rapport* established between them will produce a true and sensitive portrait.

V S-W's biographies are not all of equal value. Sometimes, as in the brief study of George Eliot, she has limited herself to too narrow a view by considering only one facet—the one that interests her—of her character. Sometimes, as with Marvell, she seems not fully to have grasped the complexity of the person she is writing about. Where she has succeeded best is where she has found most common ground with her subject—with Pepita, with the saints, and, above all, with la Grande Mademoiselle. And her best is very good indeed.

CHAPTER VIII

❦ Poetry ❦

V S-W STARTED WRITING POETRY during the Georgian Era, and by 1922, when the fifth and last volume of E.M.'s *Georgian Poetry* appeared, she had already published two volumes of her own, *Poems of West and East,* 1917, and *Orchard and Vineyard,* 1921, in addition to the two she had had privately printed.

The term "Georgian poets" has variously been used to describe those poets who wrote in the second decade of this century, to describe a poetic school, and, particularly in the years between the wars, as an uncritical term of abuse. In an admirable study of the period, Robert Ross sums up the attitude that has frequently been adopted toward the Georgian poets:

> For some years the collective reputation of the Georgians has been at a low ebb. Indeed, perhaps no group of poets since the Pre-Raphaelites has suffered more, or more ignominiously, from the widespread acceptance of over-simplified stereotypes and critical half-truths, even among readers who should know better. Often the Georgians have been misrepresented because of the ignorance of their subsequent critics, but even more often they have been the victims of pure critical spleen. Many of the major Georgian poets surely deserve rescue from the almost universal obloquy which the weaknesses of a few of the brethren have drawn down upon the heads of the entire body.

The Georgian revolt, which began about 1911, was "a part of the larger twentieth-century revolt against Humanism; in the beginning it was the poetic phase of a widespread revolt against Academism among all the arts; and, specifically in the field of poetry, it was a reaction against the dead hand of the Romantic-Victorian tradition." In their revolt against fin-de-siècle aestheticism and sentimentality, these poets turned to the primitive, the brutal, and the ugly.

This reaction against Victorianism soon divided into two main streams: one, which could accept neither the matter nor the manner of its predecessors; another, less radical, which was prepared to tolerate the matter, but was determined to find new ways of expressing it. The former was ready to trample on any convention in an effort to attain precision, and many of its members became Futurists, or Vorticists, or Imagists, as well as espousing the cause of vers libre, with Ezra Pound as one of their foremost prophets. The latter stream was reluctant to sever all connections with the past and sought for truth to life through a new realism, though frequently retaining more traditional forms of verse.

When Edward Marsh published the first two volumes of *Georgian Poetry,* in 1912 and 1915, he included a large number of vigorous poems written by the less revolutionary of these two streams. They were criticized by some reviewers for their "affected and self-conscious brutality" and for their rawness of tone, but for many poets and a large part of the reading public they were proof that poetry was at last undergoing a transformation. Beginning with the third volume, however, a change was noticeable. The old Georgians of volumes one and two began slowly to lose their dominance to Neo-Georgians, who increasingly began to set the tone of the later Georgian anthologies. "The Neo-Georgians were poets of the moon; their verse was washed white with the pale beams of Diana. Compared to the best of the Georgians the Neo-Georgians were pallid, lifeless, and monotonous. And they were to take Edward Marsh's anthology eventually from the real world of men and things, the world of truth to life, to an eternally moon-washed land of tropic nights."

One of the newcomers in the fifth, and last, volume of *Georgian Poetry,* published in 1922, was V S-W, who contributed seven poems taken from *Orchard and Vineyard.* They were not Neo-Georgian in character, but stood out by reason of their tone from much of the poetry included in the anthology. As Ross says, "with the striking exceptions of D. H. Lawrence's 'Snake,' some selections from Blunden's *The Shepherd* and *The Waggoner,* and several from Vita Sackville-West's *Orchard and Vineyard, Georgian Poetry* V contained by and large the same kind of bloodless verse which had characterized Volume IV."

The difference in tone may be illustrated by "Full Moon":

She was wearing the coral taffeta trousers
Someone had brought her from Isfahan,
And the little gold coat with pomegranate blossoms,
And the coral-hafted feather fan;
But she ran down a Kentish lane in the moonlight,
And skipped in a pool of the moon as she ran.

She cared not a rap for all the big planets,
For Betelgeuse and Aldebaran,
And all the big planets cared nothing for her.
That small impertinent charlatan,
As she climbed on a Kentish stile in the moonlight,
And laughed at the sky through the sticks of her fan.

The poet Herbert Palmer commented on this poem: "But Victoria Sackville-West's 'Full Moon' (which appeared in the fifth Georgian anthology) is rather apart from her other work, and looks like a gesture of homage to the new school. . . . A gesture of homage? But equally likely a gesture of derision: 'The small impertinent charlatan.' And it was the planets which were big and important rather than the moon. An odd, delightful, jaunty little lyric, which, in spite of its title 'Full Moon,' does *not* really get the moonlight atmosphere of the new domination, and makes no particular bow to the Man in the Moon, whether that be J. C. Squire or a mere allegorical presence."

Derisive? Probably. V S-W makes it clear in one of a series of radio talks she gave on modern poetry that "with the Georgians we are still in the company of poets who think that the poetic conventions are good enough for them; and who elect to retreat into the sanctified cloisters of the poetic paradise, taking their readers with them, rather than blunt the delicate weapons of their art against an enemy who does not play the game according to their rules." Her article on the future of the novel shows that she had little respect for competent mediocrity; her remark that the novel "is well done, certainly, but it is being done over and over and over again; repetition is death" would not apply with less force to poetry, where her critical standards were even higher.

Of V S-W's other poems in *Georgian Poetry* V, Herbert Palmer remarks: "But if Blunden is shown at his most pastoral, Victoria Sackville-West is left a little more to surmise. One of her selected poems, 'Bitterness,' is much more symbolical than is usual with Georgian poetry, and her frequent inclination to write of the passions and adventures of the human soul is somewhat at variance with her country-life aloofness."

If V S-W was influenced by the Neo-Georgians, that influence was almost certainly a negative one. She does, however, owe a debt to the older Georgians and those of their successors who revolted against the sterility of poetic diction that was widespread in the second and third decades of this century. Her attitude is illustrated in the opening sentences of a talk on Wordsworth that she delivered in 1944 to the Royal Society of Literature. To bring out his relevance in relation to modern poetry, she began by making the assumption that he was born in 1907 instead of 1770: "He was thus of just the right age by 1930 to react vigorously against the so-called Georgian School of poets [by which she almost certainly meant the Neo-Georgians]. The attitude and idiom of this school appeared to him completely outworn and divorced from reality; and . . . he proceeded boldly to outrage the accepted standards of taste and vocabulary; an attempt which met with little favour from the critics or the public, but which, considered in retrospect, can be seen now as setting up another milestone along the long road of English literature."

From a poet who makes such a declaration one would expect verse free from outworn poetic diction and in close touch with reality. One of the characteristics of much of V S-W's poetry is, in fact, its freshness of imagery and diction, based on her keen powers of observation and originality. This applies particularly to her bucolic poetry, above all to *The Land* and *The Garden*.

Contemporary poets seem to have influenced V S-W very little. T. S. Eliot, for example, early became for her almost an obsession, a symbol of pessimism and the negative outlook on life. Such was the strength of this antipathy, which seems to have been engendered by *The Waste Land,* that she was later unable to appreciate the Eliot who could offer rebirth through the death of self. In 1945, she could still write:

"April is the cruellest month, breeding
Lilacs out of the dead land, mixing
Memory and desire, stirring
Dull roots with spring rain."
Would that my pen like a blue bayonet
Might skewer all such cats'-meat of defeat;
No buttoned foil, but killing blade in hand.

The land and not the waste land celebrate,
The rich and hopeful land, the solvent land,
Not some poor desert strewn with nibbled bones,
A land of death, sterility, and stones.

The idea, and particularly the title, of *The Land,* which V S-W probably began writing in 1923, should be regarded to some extent as an answer to *The Waste Land* (1922).

Walter de la Mare was the only contemporary poet that V S-W singled out for praise. Her appreciation of him is clearly expressed in a lecture she read to the British Academy in 1953, and in a radio tribute she broadcast on the occasion of his eightieth birthday that year. Though V S-W undoubtedly admired de la Mare as a poet, she was influenced by his work very little.

Among the remarks that V S-W made about de la Mare in the Wharton Lecture is one which merits particular consideration, for it might with equal justice have been used about V S-W herself: "He is far too original and personal a poet to derive from anbody; even, I would say, to be greatly influenced."

One influence that *is* important when considering the work of V S-W is that of the Symbolists and Post-Symbolists. As early as 1926 she made it clear that she considered one of the gains to modern poetry was "a question of focus," which "was born in France where Mallarmé and Rimbaud, no less than Cézanne, began to see life from a queer, unfamiliar, oblique angle, something like a caricature, which surprises us first by its unlikeness, and then by its likeness, to the object."

Nineteenth-century Symbolism was a protest against the prevailing realism which sought to substitute scientific art for that based on lost religious values. "The Realists had no use for that belief in a superior world above the senses which has been familiar in Europe since Augustine absorbed the doctrines of Neo-Platonism; they had a stern conviction that what mattered was truth and that truth could be found empirically in this world. . . . Against this scientific Realism the Symbolists protested, and their protest was mystical in that it was made on behalf of an ideal world which was, in their judgement, more real than that of the senses. It was not in any strict sense Christian."

It is clear that V S-W had a great deal in common with the Symbolists and their successors, particularly the latter. She too resented the yoke of realism. In her article on the future of the novel, she

complained that "circumstantial detail—once so exciting a discovery—frets us now, and irritates. We are bored by the aspidistra on
the lodging-house window-sill and by the pattern on the lace curtains
shutting out the sun. Realism itself has turned into a private school-
boy's irreverent gesture rather apprehensively made under the nose
of Lord Brentford." There is also, as we have already seen, a strong
vein of neo-platonism and pantheism in her writing, particularly in
later years. Finally, she frequently made use of symbols, both in her
poetry and prose, although she seems to have kept mainly to traditional ones, such as Olver's distorting mirror in *Grey Wethers* and the
symbol of the rose in *The Garden.*

The two extremes of poetry are instruction on the one hand and
magic on the other. The Post-Symbolists, in contrast to some of the
Symbolists, "accept the fact that words have meanings and that poetry
must be understood." But as Maurice Bowra points out, "they have
none the less kept to the magical view of it. They aim at moving hearts
and stirring imaginations." This is an outlook that V S-W shares with
them. In her works, the magical is most evident in her novels, for example in *Grey Wethers, Seducers in Ecuador, Grand Canyon,* and in several of her short stories, particularly "Gottfried Künstler."

Above all, however, V S-W was "a poet in a tradition," and fully
aware of the fact that she was writing in a tradition regarded as obso-
lete by many people who "suffer from the delusion that the possibili-
ties of bucolic poetry are dead." In the poem "Sissinghurst," she
refers to herself as

> A tired swimmer in the waves of time
> I throw my hands up: let the surface close:
> Sink down through centuries to another clime,
> And buried find the castle and the rose . . .
> And here, by birthright far from present fashion,
> As no disturber of the mirrored trance
> I move, and to the world above the waters
> Wave my incognisance.

She has also referred to herself as "a damned out-moded poet." This
awareness was partially responsible for the periods of depression
from which she sometimes suffered and may also be the explanation
why inspiration fails to illuminate some of her less successful poems.
On the other hand, this sense of belonging to a tradition was also the
source of much of her great strength; it was so deeply ingrained in

her that, when asked about how she had written *The Land,* she was able to reply, "I had not read the Georgics until half of my own poem had been written, and then a friend to whom I showed it spoke of the resemblance, so after that I read it."

V S-W's affinity to tradition is apparent in her diction and vocabulary no less than in her choice of subject matter and form. The style in which she chooses to write her poetry is a simple and clear one, and although these are fundamental qualities of her nature, the choice was probably deliberate. Echoes of Shakespeare are constantly to be met with in her poetry, above all, perhaps, in metrical cadences which carry the mind direct to him. Who, for example, can read

> . . . He knows, he knows
> The disappointments, the discomfitures,
> The waste, the dash of hopes, the sweet surprise
> Sprung in forgotten corner; knows the loss,
> Attempts defeated, optimism balked;
> He may not pause to lean upon his spade.

without hearing the cadences of

> For who would bear the whips and scorns of time,
> The oppressor's wrong, the proud man's contumely,
> The pangs of despised love, the law's delay,
> The insolence of office and the spurns
> That patient merit of the unworthy takes.

As regards form, she clearly also owes more than a little to Thomson, particularly as she began to write *The Land* without having read Virgil; and John Clare and Edward Thomas are her immediate precursors.

Turning to a consideration of individual poems, a remark made by Richard Church provides an excellent introduction. She is, he said, "another poet given to the exploration of solitude, to a private agony, and its assuagement in the delights of the soil." The subjective lyricism which characterizes her shorter poems up to and including 1933, the year in which she published *Collected Poems,* is nakedly passionate, intensely personal, and filled with unrest. Given its head, this tendency toward the unleashing of violent emotions led, in some of her unpublished poems, to detrimental excesses. What saved her in the nineteen-twenties was the strength of tradition and the fact that she wrote *The Land.* In later years, she turned to religious speculation and wrote biographies, both of which had a steadying influence on her style.

The Land was in several respects a turning point in her poetic career. In deciding to write this long poem she was, at the same time, making a decision to subject herself to a discipline more rigorous than had been necessary for any of her shorter poems. A work on the scale of *The Land* demanded an objectivity, a precision, and a degree of planning far in excess of anything she had hitherto been compelled to employ. There can be little doubt that she gained immensely by having to do so.

To head the completed poem, V S-W chose two lines from *The Georgics:*

Nec sum animi dubius, verbis ea vincere magnum
quam sit et angustis hunc addere rebus honorem.

Commenting on her choice of a heading, Richard Church says: "Through that restriction of theme, however, she has mastered more than her subject. She has mastered also the waywardness and turbulence of her moods, brought down their vagueness to a precision that is hard and objective, given them a universal out of a personal value. She has put her hand to the plough in more senses than one. She says that 'the country habit has me by the heart,' and her heart, under that discipline, works the more harmoniously with her mind. This process, a hard one which cannot be mastered merely by willing, needs time, patience and experience before it can be acquired. Once acquired, however, it produces that essential poetry which is content with simple words, unliterary associations, and humble effects."

In the middle of the nineteen-thirties, when her thoughts began to turn to religious speculation, V S-W abandoned novel writing for a form that again required rigid discipline, namely biography. The need once more to marshal her thoughts and govern her emotions must have been an exercise that was beneficial to her poetry too, for her last poems, *Solitude* (1938) and *The Garden* (1946), show a control absent in some of her previous works.

The Land and *The Garden* are probably the two poems on which V S-W will be judged by posterity. *The Land* has almost a double validity for, apart from its poetic worth, it is a record of a rural culture that has governed the lives of a great number of Englishmen for several hundred years, but which was already fast disappearing when she

Wartime poetry reading, 1943. Seated, from left to right: Edith Sitwell, Gordon Bottomley, V. Sackville-West, Arthur Waley, and John Masefield.

wrote the poem. L. A. G. Strong recollects that he "heard farmers discussing Miss Sackville-West's long poem *The Land,* not as poetry, but as a manual of country matters. This in itself would be no commendation . . . but, taken in conjunction with the fact that *The Land* was immediately acclaimed by poets, it means a great deal."

On its first appearance it was hailed with almost universal approval by the critics, the one notable exception being Edith Sitwell, who, replying to a statement by John Drinkwater that *The Land* contained some of the loveliest verse written in this century, retorted: "Well, *I* can only say that it does *not.* I am told by competent persons that Miss Sackville-West's prose is charming. It seems, therefore, a distinct pity to put it into metre. The book would probably be of great use to prospective farmers, for it is one long catalogue of agricultural implements, and the right way to do everything,—to 'stook' (whatever that may mean), and to thatch. The book tells you exactly when and how to reap and cut everything that grows. It also mentions birds' nests and Helen's breast." However, when Edith Sitwell published her anthology of verse, *The Atlantic Book of British and American Poetry,* in 1958, it contained a five-page-long extract from *The Land*—only one page less than she devoted to Thomas Hardy, and considerably more

From *The Land.*

From the first draft of *The Garden.*

than was allotted to Emerson, Housman, or D. H. Lawrence. The extract included a reference to birds' nests and to Helen's breast.

Grierson and Smith emphasize another aspect of the poem. "There is," they point out, "no false pastoralism about the pictures, nor yet the bitter realism of Crabbe: the land is a hard task-mistress, but a just one. *The Land* (1926) is a refreshing poem, more like Hesiod perhaps than Virgil, with something of the eighteenth century in its cool good sense."

Richard Church's opinion is quite clear: "During the war I wrote a critical essay in the *Fortnightly Review*, which was then collected into book form . . . and published by Dents under the title *Eight for Immortality*. . . . As the title suggests, my view of her poetry is that it is in the permanent tradition and is likely to endure the criticism of time when more fashionable verse has been forgotten."

The Garden has received much less critical attention than *The Land*. In part this is probably due to the fact that V S-W died just about the time when second thoughts about the poem might have been expected. Partly, perhaps, it may be that critics felt as a lack what V S-W herself experienced as a difficulty when she was writing the poem. "It is much more difficult than *The Land,* because the inherent dignity of agriculture is lacking, and seed-boxes are not so romantic as tilth." And partly it may be because it is, by reason of the underlying speculation on religion and death, a far more personal poem than *The Land.* Whatever the reason, *The Garden,* which was very well received on publication, has not shown the same ability as *The Land* to capture the imagination of the public; it has not yet been reprinted, although the first edition of 15,000 copies sold out in September 1961. Whatever the cause, in this long poem in the English tradition in which "never stretching thought or language beyond the range which comes to her naturally, she accomplishes a quiet perfection from restrained poetic speech which is likely to be listened to after louder and more singular voices have wearied their audience."

V S-W's poetry will never reach a wide public; it is too deeply rooted in tradition and too personal to do that. But, for those very reasons, neither will it be forgotten.

❦ Conclusion ❧

IT MUST BE VERY RARE for a poet of renown also to be a distinguished biographer as well as a good novelist. V S-W was all three. She also wrote books on gardening, about which her knowledge was impressive, which may be, and are, read for the sheer pleasure of reading them.

V S-W was never a professional author in the sense that she wrote in order to earn her daily bread. With the possible exception of the years between 1930 and 1936 she had no need to do so. The principal reason why she wrote was certainly the creative urge common to all artists, but in part it seems also to have been due to an inner compulsion to set down on paper in some transmuted form the problems and doubts which beset her. V S-W's acute consciousness of her mixed ancestry, her upbringing under her mother, her difficulty in establishing contact with people, and other factors produced a duality in her nature which she does not seem to have overcome until she was over fifty years of age. Later in life, partly perhaps through the influence of her sister-in-law, her thoughts turned to religion, in which she sought, not consolation, but an explanation of the contradictions in life she could not but notice around her. She would have wished to be granted faith, the ability to believe wholeheartedly in Christianity or some other religion, but there is no evidence that such faith ever came to her.

She therefore resorted to an artistic medium in order to explain her difficulties to herself, and the result was literature, both in prose and poetry.

This should not for a moment be taken to imply that an inner compulsion arising out of personal problems was the sole source of her inspiration. The best of her work, both in poetry and in prose, owes far more to her native originality, a sense of the traditions of literature, psychological insight, an acute power of observation, a natural gift of style, and a feeling for language. When she had learnt to discipline her turbulent emotions, which she did by forcing herself to work within a rigidly fixed scheme, she was able to write works of great power and simplicity, such as *The Land.*

Vita Sackville-West was a particular sort of person who lived at a particular moment in time. By an accident of birth, she belonged to a class many members of which were not able to take part in the social struggle that was rife in Europe. The detachment this gave her renders her free from a sense of urgency, and she was little influenced by the sound and fury around her. It also enabled her to keep her eyes fixed on the eternal values that her feeling for tradition told her were the essential ones, for, as she has said, she felt "a lack of interest in what must always be temporary things, things that in a thousand years' time will have become meaningless." This is why she could also say "neither do I feel attracted to *la poésie engagée.*" It becomes dated all too soon.

This detachment, however, did not mean that she did not observe. She both observed and recorded, and the record is the more valuable for the detachment. There can be little doubt that V S-W regarded many of the phenomena of modern life with distaste; her private correspondence bears witness to that. But in her art she never condemns any but her peers.

To her art V S-W brought a real poetic gift. But her attitude toward her muse was one of great humility. "You know," she wrote to H.N., "I do get so frightfully, frenziedly excited writing poetry. It is the only thing that makes me truly and completely happy. And then I feel that what I have been writing is so very poor—so wretched a reflection of what has been going on in my mind while I am at it. Why should one rise so high and then go so completely flop?"

V. Sackville-West at Sissinghurst.

APPENDIX A

"A Question of Inspiration"

THE OTHER DAY we received the following letter from a correspondent:

Sir,—In Clifford Dyment's new book, *Poems 1935–1948,* there is included the following poem:

SAINT AUGUSTINE AT 32
Girl, why do you follow me
When I come to the threshold of the holy place?
My resolution falters: it seems a death to enter
When, turning back, I look into your face.
I saw you when I lay alone
And ran from you as from a searching light
Into the gentle, acquiescent
Obscurity of the night.
I crave communion that is not words
And life fulfilled in my cell alone—
And you, you come with your lips and your gold hair
And at your feet is a leaf that the wind has blown.

The lines struck me as familiar. I turned up the *Poetry Review* of June—July, 1949, and there read:

THE NOVICE TO HER LOVER
Why must you follow me
When I come to the threshold of this holy place?
My resolution falters and it seems death to enter
When, turning back, I look upon your face.
I could renounce you when I lay alone;
I ran from you as from a hungry light

Into the gentle, the infinite, the healing
Clemency of the night.
I crave an eloquence that is not words,
I seek fulfilment in the kiss of stone—
But you, you come with your mouth and your dark hair
And at your feet a leaf that the wind has blown.

V. Sackville-West

In Mr. Dyment's book his poem is dated 1944. I therefore consulted his 1944 volume, *The Axe in the Wood,* and there found the poem in a version even nearer Miss Sackville-West's. The mystery of the parallel between the two poems has puzzled me. I am unable to find any explanation. Can any of your readers?

Leonard Hickman

Clearly, Mr. Hickman raised a fascinating question. But perhaps there was a simple explanation—for instance, that both Mr. Dyment and Miss Sackville-West had, unknown to each other, adapted or translated some earlier poem. So, before printing Mr. Hickman's letter, we decided to send a copy to the poets themselves.

From Mr. Dyment we had this reply:

Yes, I have heard about the extraordinarily puzzling similarity between the two poems, as Miss Sackville-West herself wrote to me about it. I am as mystified as she is. All I know is that my poem was first published in January, 1943, in the *St. Martin's Review* and subsequently reprinted in book form in 1944 and 1949, and that it is not a translation. I think it would be very interesting if Mr. Hickman's letter were published, as it might bring forward other cases of the same sort of thing. It's all very odd.

And from Miss Sackville-West:

The facts, so far as I am concerned, are:
(a) I wrote my poem *The Novice to her Lover* some time in 1942 or early in 1943, when I was engaged on an essay * about St. Thérèse of Lisieux, the "novice" I had in mind. I put the poem away and thought no more about it. I did not even get it typed, and no one saw it except one person, to whom, as a recently converted Catholic and a devotee of St. Thérèse, I sent it embodied in a letter. I have now made inquiries from this person, who assures me that she neither showed the poem to anyone, nor caused any copy of it to be made. Thus, no one but myself and this one other person had seen my poem, until—

* Published in *The Eagle and the Dove,* 1943.

(*b*) The *Poetry Review* wrote to ask me for some unpublished verses of mine for their Jubilee numbers in the summer of 1949. I then looked through my MSS. Book; I found this poem; and they duly printed it.

(*c*) In November, 1949, I borrowed a copy of Mr. Dyment's *Poems,* published by Messrs. Dent, and therein read with some astonishment a poem which I recognised as almost identical with a poem of my own.

(*d*) I then immediately wrote to Mr. Dyment who, I felt, must be as puzzled as I. He agreed that he was; but reminded me of a letter I had written him in 1944, in reference to his book of poems entitled *The Axe in the Wood,* of which he had sent me a copy through his publishers, Messrs. Dent, and in which his poem *St. Augustine at* 32 was included. It seems that in my letter to Mr. Dyment I singled out this poem for especial praise. The whole story becomes less and less explicable.

Why did I not recognise my own poem in Mr. Dyment's volume in 1944?

Why did I recognise it at once in Mr. Dyment's volume in 1949?

How did Mr. Dyment and I come to write the same poem, in a rather unusual metre, about two very different saints, at approximately the same time, i.e. 1942 or 1943?

It is of course, unthinkable that either I or Mr. Dyment should have "lifted" a poem from one another. That supposition can be dismissed. But what, then, is the explanation?

I have none to offer.

Have our readers any explanation? Or knowledge of any similar instances of the same inspiration visiting two poets?

And what if all of animated nature
Be but organic Harps diversely fram'd,
That tremble into thought, as o'er them sweep
Plastic and vast, one intellectual breeze . . .

Is this an illustration of the poet acting, as Coleridge believed he might, as an Aeolian harp? Or is there a less romantic explanation, such as a common source in some book of memoirs or devotions which both poets had read and both forgotten?

From the *New Statesman and Nation,* 21 January 1950, p. 62.

Clifford Dyment died in June 1971. The year after, a friend of his, Robert Greacen, published a memoir to Dyment in *Encounter* which contains the following passage:

There is a literary curiosity in which Clifford was involved. He wrote a poem called "St. Augustine at 32" and then, later, Victoria Sackville-West published almost exactly the same poem under her own name. This is what Clifford has to say about it:

"Victoria Sackville-West and I might have drawn from a common unconscious source. The Society for Psychical Research looked into it and newspapers carried the story on their first pages headed 'Piddington Act Among the Poets'—the Piddingtons being famous mind-readers of the time, 1950. However all that may be, the facts, briefly, are these: in 1949 I published 'St. Augustine at 32' in a volume of my own poems; also, in 1949, Victoria Sackville-West published the poem, as hers, in *The Poetry Review*. The two poems were almost exactly the same except in title and sex of the subject, mine concerning a monk and hers a nun. As far as I know the episode is unique in literature: there are cases of two authors writing identical lines but not identical complete poems. However, I must add that my 'St. Augustine' had appeared in print twice before 1949—in 1943 and 1944. These complications, and explanatory theories, are discussed by Robin Skelton in his book *The Poetic Pattern* and in a paper by the late Professor Edwin G. Bering in an American book called *Readings for Introductory Psychology*."

The whole business upset Clifford very much and he believed—perhaps wrongly—that he had suffered in reputation as a result. . . . I could never get him to tell me why he didn't insist on meeting V. Sackville-West and discussing the matter.

APPENDIX B

ॐ Unpublished Poems ॐ

In December 1963 I visited Sissinghurst Castle and was allowed to spend several days in V S-W's study in the tower examining the papers which, according to Nigel Nicolson, no one had touched up to that time. On the writing desk and in briefcases and files around and under it were the first and second drafts of *The Garden,* the first or second drafts of eighty-three published poems, and the drafts of one hundred and ninety-seven unpublished poems, as well as a number of brief prose drafts on various subjects. From this material the following unpublished poems have been selected to illustrate some facets of V S-W's personality.

Contact with beauty, for me, is direct and immediate.
The sight of beauty, for me, is the meaning of beauty.
I do not get the meaning at a second remove.
An ocean, a landscape, or a lovely woman
Are immediate and complete experiences.
A tree in winter, bare, without the loveliness
Of leaves, a tree bare to its branches
Lovelier far than dressed in summer beauty.
I like things stripped down to truth,
Un-prettied, unromanticised.

DIARY POEM
My heart is broken against grey stone,
Against the Kentish Rag.
Smashed against it as ships in wreck
Smash on a Cornish crag.

Cracked is my heart and cannot mend;
It broke twelve years ago;

Never, never, never again
Shall I call my heart my own.

My heart was torn from my broken breast
And thrown against the stone—
The stone of my own friendly home
That broke it in the end.

Never, never, never to mend;
A smash that never heals;
Oh sorrow, that the thing I love
Should be the thing that kills.

Knole, you would not have broken me?
Me, passionate and wild?
You loved me, surely, in so far
As stone can love its child?

Knole, when I went from you, you missed
One of your many children, specially?
God knows I gave you all my love, my agony,
Scarcely a stone of you I had not kissed.

Knole! Knole! I stretch my hands to you in prayer,
You, grey and solid; you, enduring, staid;
You do not know what surges beat against your walls;
Miss me a little, I who am your soul.

DIARY POEM
I look at my name on an envelope:
The Hon. Mrs Harold Nicolson
In beautiful legal type
From my solicitor's office
Enclosing a legal form
For the purchase of land in Kent.

Then I look at my other name,
My own my personal name,
The name my ancestors gave to me,
The name I have kept for myself.

And it seems to me that the name I bore
Is better adapted to lands in Kent
Than the Scottish name my sons must bear,
For my son has gone to the Western Isles,
My son has gone to the Hebrides,
My son doesn't give a damn for Kent,

But I was bred from Sussex and Kent,
And my name is dear to me.

I will hold to my own, old name,
Walled within walls of Knole;
I will not sink my pride, my soul,
In another's pride and fame.

I have pride enough of my own, thank God,
And I have earned my right
To be no tin can on another's tail,—
Rattle, and dragged about.

My proudest boast: I will give my love
Stintless, with all its pain;
But my name is mine, and my lands in Kent
Should be mine, like my books, in name.

HEREDITY

What is this thing, this bond,
That brings us here together?
That keeps us, though we roam,
All on a length of tether?

Why are our faces cut
All in the same sad feature?
It is a quirk, a trick
Played on us all by Nature.

I am not you, I am I;
Nothing is foreordained.
I hold my liberty
Unstained and unconstrained.

Because I have your eyes
Does it mean I have your heart?
No, you are you, I am I,
Independent and apart.

Violently I refuse
All seisin with another,
Be she my kinswoman,
Be he my own blood-brother.

—Yet stay. Had he that lies
Dead in the chapel, not

The same unhappy eyes?
My father, that me begot?

Yet stay. Have they not all,
The portraits in gilded frame,
Upstairs, the same sad pensive look
The same, and still the same?

What is this thing, this strain,
Persistent, what this shape
That cuts us from our birth,
And seals without escape?

Long Barn, 16 February 1928

I suppose other people endure the same dissatisfactions—
I suppose they all think that nobody understands them;
I suppose they think that words are no good, and that anyway one can
never say what one means.
That is where sex comes in, the arch-deceiver.
Sex deludes one into the belief that one has attained real contact with
another person;
And since the horrible loneliness of the soul makes one crave for some
contact,
One turns gratefully to sex as a short-cut to contact.
But it isn't true, it isn't true; yet what is true?
Is it true, ever, to say "I love!" with its implications,
Knowing that the truth wears quite a different face for oneself or an-
other?
Yes, it may be true to say "I love," but in the last resort
There is no possibility of contact, except in a brief delusion.

Is it true, ever true, to say "I love"?
Yes, it can, I believe, be true.
It is true when the concerns of other people matter to me more than my
own concerns,
When there is no selfishness involved.
When I mind, vitally, in myself, if they are cold or warm,
Whether they catch their train or have to linger on platforms;
Whether they meet with applause or a snub in their undertakings;
If these things matter, then, in my innermost self
As though they affected myself, then I know I love.

LITANY: I AM

I am the snail
    crawling out at night to devour the flower.

I am the flower devoured by the snail—
I am the lion in his desert
I am the gazelle brought down by the lion—
I am the dog who lies down by man's hearth.

I am the horse—who was once no bigger than a hare
    but who now pulls men's carriages and farm-waggons.
I have grown to the Suffolk Punch and the Percheron—
I am the man
I am the star—the black dwarf
I am the Galaxy
I am the speed of light
I am the atom. I am the atom bomb.
I am the Universe, receding so fast that no telescope
    can catch up with it
I AM, because I think I am.

And now my dog comes and pokes me with his nose, saying it's time for me to have my dinner.

APPENDIX C

❧ Published Works ❦

POETRY

WORK	REPRINTED IN
Chatterton: A Drama in Three Acts, J. Salmon, Sevenoaks, 1909 (Privately printed).	
"The Dancing Elf," *The English Review,* XV (August 1913).	*Poems of West and East*
Constantinople, Complete Press, London, 1915 (Privately printed).	*Poems of West and East*
Poems of West and East, John Lane, London, 1917.	*Collected Poems*
"Ad Astra," *The Anglo-French Review,* III (June 1920), 468–9.	*Orchard and Vineyard*
"Escape," *The Anglo-French Review,* III (June 1920), 496.	*Orchard and Vineyard*
"A Fallen Soldier," *Observer,* 5 June 1921.	*Orchard and Vineyard*
"Sorrow of Departure," *Observer,* 5 June 1921.	*Orchard and Vineyard*
"Evening," London *Mercury,* IV (September 1921), 467.	*Orchard and Vineyard*
Orchard and Vineyard, John Lane, London, 1921.	*Collected Poems*
"Winter Song," London *Mercury,* VII (December 1922), 128–9.	*The Land*
"Alice Meynell," *Observer,* 17 December 1922.	*Collected Poems*
"Moonlight," London *Mercury,* VIII (May 1923).	
"Song," London *Mercury,* VIII (May 1923).	*Collected Poems*
"Making Cider," London *Mercury,* VIII (October 1923), 567.	*The Land*
"The Bee-Master," London *Mercury,* VIII (October 1923), 568–70.	*The Land*
"Sea Sonnet," *Poetry Review,* VIII (December 1923).	*Collected Poems*

"Tuscany," London *Mercury,* IX (March 1924),
  461–2.   *The Land*
"The Island," *Nation and Athenaeum,* XXXVI (March
  1925), 776.   *The Land*
"Woodcraft," London *Mercury,* XI (April 1925).   *The Land*
"On the Lake," *Nation and Athenaeum,* XXXVIII (De-
  cember 1925), 469.   *Collected Poems*
The Land, William Heinemann, London, 1926.   *Collected Poems*
"Winter," *New Paths on Helicon,* Thomas Nelson,
  London, 1927.
"Black Tarn," London *Mercury,* XV (March 1927).   *Collected Poems*
"At Rhey," *Bermondsey Book,* IV (June 1927).   *Collected Poems*
"In Syria," *Literary Digest,* XCV (October 1927),
  New York.   *Collected Poems*
"Palmyra," *Time and Tide,* IX (17 February 1928).   *Collected Poems*
"Love Song," *Time and Tide,* IX (9 March 1928), 224.   *Collected Poems*
"Eclipse," *Daily Express,* 27 July 1928.
"Bowl of Blue Beads," *Daily Express,* 22 October
  1928.   *Collected Poems*
"Idyll," *Time and Tide,* X (10 March 1929).   *King's Daughter*
"Nocturne," *Listener,* I (13 March 1929), 327.
"Illusions," London *Mercury,* XX (October 1929),
  556.   *King's Daughter*
King's Daughter, Hogarth Press, London, 1929.   *Collected Poems*
"Poem," *Time and Tide,* X (8 November 1929), 1338.
"Storm in the Mountains," London *Mercury,* XXI
  (December 1929).   *Collected Poems*
"Peace in the Mountains," *Poetry Review,* XXI (Jan-
  uary 1930).   *Collected Poems*
"Persia," *Spectator,* CXLVI (31 January 1931).   *Collected Poems*
"Chanson Perpetuelle," *Listener,* V (10 June 1931),
  981.   *Collected Poems*
Rilke, *Duineser Elegien,* trans. (with Edward Sackville-
  West), Hogarth Press, London, 1931.
Sissinghurst, Hogarth Press, London, 1931.   *Collected Poems*
Invitation To Cast Out Care, Faber & Faber, London,
  1931.   *Collected Poems*
"Reddín," *A Miscellany of Verse Never Before Published,*
  Victor Gollancz, London, 1931.   *Collected Poems*
"A Dream," *Week-end Review,* IV (5 December 1931).   *Collected Poems*
"Encounter," *Week-end Review,* V (5 January 1932).   *Collected Poems*
"Absence," *Week-end Review,* V (26 March 1932).   *Collected Poems*
"The Bull," *Week-end Review,* VI (1 October 1932).   *Collected Poems*
"To Any M.F.H.," *Review of Reviews,* LXXXV (Jan-
  uary 1933).   *Collected Poems*
Collected Poems, Hogarth Press, London, 1933, Dou-
  bleday, Doran, New York, 1934.

"December Night," *New Statesman and Nation,* XII (5 December 1936), 892–3.

Solitude, Hogarth Press, London, 1938, Doubleday, Doran, New York, 1939.

"Winter Afternoon," *Times Literary Supplement,* 5 November 1938.

"Reminiscence," *Listener,* XXI (23 March 1939).

"Gas-Proof Room," *New Statesman and Nation,* XVIII (2 December 1939).

"Prayer in the Desert," *Observer,* 10 December 1939.

"Appeal," *St. Martin's Review,* March 1940.

"Personal Valour," *Observer,* 23 June 1940.

"July, 1940," *Observer,* 21 July 1940.

"In Memoriam: Virginia Woolf," *Observer,* 6 April 1941.

Selected Poems, Hogarth Press, London, 1941.

"August, 1941," *Observer,* 24 August 1941.

"The Comet," *Times Literary Supplement,* 17 April 1943.

"On a Dutch Flower Picture," *Spectator,* CLXXI (31 December 1943).   *The Garden*

"Blast," *Observer,* 23 April 1944.

"Ethel Smythe," *Observer,* 14 May 1944.

"Spitfire and Flying Bomb," *Observer,* 25 June 1944.

"Les Français parlent aux Français," *Times Literary Supplement,* 15 July 1944.

"This War Will Soon Be Over," *Observer,* 14 May 1944.   *The Garden*

"The Crater in the Field," *Country Life,* XCVI (8 September 1944).   *The Garden*

"Searchlights," *Times Literary Supplement,* 16 September 1944.   *The Garden*

"Blackout," *Observer,* 8 October 1944.   *The Garden*

"Dog," *Country Life,* XCVI (27 October 1944).

"Stone Manger," *Times Literary Supplement,* 23 December, 1944, p. 620.   *The Garden*

"Nativity," *New Statesman and Nation,* XXX (22 December 1945).   *The Garden*

"You Happy Baby at the Cottage Door," *Decachord,* XXIII (January–February 1946).

The Garden, Michael Joseph, London, Doubleday, New York, 1946.

"Ellen Terry," London *Times,* 27 February 1947.

"The Novice to Her Lover," *Poetry Review,* XL (June 1949).

"June 2nd, 1953," *Times Literary Supplement,* 5 June 1953, p. 358.

ANTHOLOGIES IN WHICH POEMS BY V S-W
ARE INCLUDED

Georgian Poetry, Vol. V, ed. E. M. (Edward Marsh), The Poetry Bookshop, London, 1922.

    "A Saxon Song," from *Orchard and Vineyard*
    "Mariana in the North"   "   "   "
    "Full Moon"   "   "   "
    "Sailing Ships"   "   "   "
    "Trio"   "   "   "
    "Bitterness"   "   "   "
    "Evening"   "   "   "

Oxford Book of Modern Verse, ed. W. B. Yeats, Oxford, 1936.

    "Greater Cats," from *King's Daughter*
    "On the Lake," from *Collected Poems*

Modern Verse in English, ed. David Cecil and Allen Tate, London, 1958.

    "On the Lake," from *Collected Poems*
    "A Dream," from *Collected Poems*

The Atlantic Book of British and American Poetry, II, ed. Edith Sitwell, London, 1959.

    "The spring was late that year," from *The Land*

Georgian Poetry, ed. James Reeves, Penguin Books, London, 1962.

    "Full Moon," from *Orchard and Vineyard*

FICTION

WORK	REPRINTED IN
Heritage, Collins, London, Doran, New York, 1919.	
The Dragon in Shallow Waters, Collins, London, 1921, Putnam, New York, 1922.	
The Heir, Heinemann, London, Doran, New York, 1922 (short stories).	
Challenge, G. Doran, New York, 1923.	
Grey Wethers, Heinemann, London, Doran, New York, 1923.	
"To Be Let or Sold," *Morning Post,* 14 December 1923 (short story).	
Seducers in Ecuador, Hogarth Press, London, 1924, Doran, New York, 1925.	
The Edwardians, Hogarth Press, London, Doubleday, Doran, New York, 1930.	
"Liberty," *Harper's Bazaar,* October 1930, pp. 44–45, 102, 104 (short story).	
"The Engagement," *Tatler,* 22 October 1930, pp. 186 and xiv (short story).	
"The Unborn Visitant," *Graphic,* Christmas Number, October 1930, pp. 22, 23, 34, 36 (short story).	*Thirty Clocks Strike the Hour*

All Passion Spent, Hogarth Press, London, Doubleday,
    Doran, New York, 1931.
"Elizabeth Higginbottom," *Spectator,* CXLVII (21 November   *Thirty Clocks*
    1931), 613–4 (short story).   *Strike the Hour*
The Death of Noble Godavary, Ernest Benn, London,   *Thirty Clocks*
    1932.   *Strike the Hour*
Family History, Hogarth Press, London, Doubleday, Doran,
    New York, 1932.
Thirty Clocks Strike the Hour, Doubleday, Doran, New York,
    1932.
"The Strange Adventures of Mr. Petherick," *Harper's Bazaar,*
    April 1933, pp. 28, 29, 92.
The Dark Island, Hogarth Press, London, Doubleday, Doran,
    New York, 1934.
Grand Canyon, Michael Joseph, London, 1942.
Devil at Westease, Doubleday, New York, 1947.
The Easter Party, Michael Joseph, London, Doubleday, New
    York, 1953.
No Signposts in the Sea, Michael Joseph, London, Doubleday,
    New York, 1961.
"Interlude in Two Lives," *Woman's Own,* 24 March 1962, pp.
    9, 83–89 and 30 March, 1962, pp. 57–69.

NON-FICTION

Knole and the Sackvilles, William Heinemann, London, 1922.
"Why women novelists neglect men," *Daily Express,* 14 January 1922.
The Diary of Lady Anne Clifford, ed. V S-W with a long preface by V S-W.
    William Heinemann, London, 1923.
"Fashions in Decoration," *Vogue,* London, April 1924, p. 61.
"On being photographed," *Evening Standard,* 15 May 1924.
"On friends and relations," *Evening Standard,* 30 May 1924.
"Mme. Dieulafoy," *Vogue,* London, June 1925, pp. 77, 112.
"Travelling in Italy," *Nation and Athenaeum,* XXXVII (Travel Number, 1925),
    3–4.
"The Garden and the Oast," *Nation and Athenaeum,* XXXVIII (10 October
    1925), 47–8.
"Gertrude Bell in Bagdad," *Nation and Athenaeum,* XXXIX (24 July 1926).
Passenger to Teheran, Hogarth Press, London, 1926.
"Gulistan," *Nation and Athenaeum,* XXXIX (10 July 1926), 413–4.
"Migration," *Nation and Athenaeum,* XLI (25 June 1927), 411–2.
"Some Tendencies of Modern English Poetry," *Essays by Divers Hands,* VII
    (1927), Royal Society of Literature, London (lecture).
Aphra Behn, Gerald Howe, London, 1927, Viking Press, New York, 1928.
"The Wit and the Wanderer," *Nation and Athenaeum,* XLIII (16 June 1928),
    358–9 (article on Dr. Johnson and Psalmanazar).

"Strange Adventures," *Time and Tide,* IX (13 July 1928), 679–80.

"Civilized Subterfuges," *Vanity Fair,* July 1928, pp. 33, 80.

"Tolstoy," *Nation and Athenaeum,* XLIII (8 September 1928), 729–30.

Twelve Days, Hogarth Press, London, Doubleday, Doran, New York, 1928.

"On poetry today," *Radio Times,* 2 November 1928, pp. 289–90.

"Four English poets of our own time," *Radio Times,* 9 November 1928, pp. 362–3.

"Modern poetry is not prose," *Radio Times,* 23 November 1928, pp. 515–6.

"The formidable Mr. Eliot," *Radio Times,* 30 November 1928, pp. 589, 628.

"The Ukraine," *Life and Letters,* December 1928, pp. 575–9.

"Multitude or solitude?," *Daily Chronicle,* 5 December 1928.

"The double existence of the Sitwells," *Radio Times,* 14 December 1928, pp. 728–9.

"There are many fine poets today," *Radio Times,* 18 January 1929, pp. 127, 130.

"Marriage," *Listener,* I (26 June 1929), 899–900.

Andrew Marvell, Faber & Faber, London, 1929.

"The Georgians," *Daily Mail,* 14 July 1930.

"Youth is perplexed," *Daily Mail,* 21 July 1930.

"The future of the novel," *Week-end Review,* II (October 1930), 535, 537. *Bookman,* New York, LXXII (December 1930), 350–1.

"Life in a cloud of ink," *Graphic,* 27 December 1930, p. 567.

"Women in literature," *Woman's Leader,* XXII (2 January 1931), 363.

"The Edwardians below stairs," *Vogue,* 25 November 1931, pp. 55–7.

"Preface" to Walther Berendsohn, *Selma Lagerlöf: her life and work,* trans. George Timson, Nicholson & Watson, London, 1931.

"George Eliot," *The Great Victorians,* ed. Massingham, Nicholson & Watson, London, 1932.

"Memory—good and bad," *Spectator,* CIL (30 July 1932).

"Ghosts," *Nash's,* December 1932, p. 52.

"Now I am a millionaire," *Nash's,* January 1933, p. 68.

"On being beautiful," *Nash's,* May 1933, p. 5.

"Our future beckons," *Pictorial Review,* XXXV (November 1933), 19, 37.

"On being unpunctual," *Everyman,* 1 December 1933.

"Elizabethan Lyrics and Metaphysical Poetry," Lord Northcliffe Lectures, 1934 (six lectures delivered at the University of London; MSS in the possession of Nigel Nicolson, Sissinghurst Castle).

"V. Sackville-West," *Beginnings,* ed. L. A. G. Strong, Thomas Nelson, London, 1935.

Saint Joan of Arc, Cobden, Sanderson, London, Doubleday, Doran, New York, 1936.

Some Flowers, Cobden, Sanderson, London, 1937.

Pepita, Hogarth Press, London, Doubleday, Doran, New York, 1937.

"W.H. Hudson: Naturalist and poet," *Listener,* XIX (2 June 1938), 1193–4.

"Vivisection," *New Statesman and Nation,* XVI (3 December 1938), 913–4.

Country Notes, Michael Joseph, London, 1939, Harper, New York, 1940.

"Hilda Matheson," *Spectator,* CLXV (22 November 1940).

Country Notes in Wartime, Michael Joseph, London, 1940, Doubleday, Doran, New York, 1941.
"Virginia Woolf," *Horizon,* III (May 1941).
English Country Houses, Collins, London, 1941.
"Knole," *Spectator,* CLXXI (15 October 1943), 356.
The Eagle and the Dove, Michael Joseph, London, 1943, Doubleday, Doran, New York, 1944.
"Progress in Persia," *Vogue,* January 1944, pp. 48–9, 67.
"Sharawadji," *Spectator,* CLXXII (14 January 1944), 29.
"Shepetovka," *Spectator,* CLXXII (25 February 1944), 169.
The Women's Land Army, Michael Joseph, London, 1944.
"Delight in Gardens," *Listener,* XXXIII (22 March 1945), 327–8.
"Wordsworth, especially in relation to modern poetry," *Essays by Divers Hands,* XXII (1945), Royal Society of Literature, London (lecture).
Another World Than This, ed. V S-W and Harold Nicolson, Michael Joseph, London, 1945 (occasional book).
"Introduction" to *Alice Meynell: Prose and Poetry,* ed. F.P., V.M., O.S., & F.M., Jonathan Cape, London, 1947.
Nursery Rhymes, Dropmore Press, London, 1947.
"Gertrude Bell," *Listener,* XL (2 December 1948), 852–3.
"Bees under my bonnet," *Time and Tide,* XXX (3 December 1949), 1212.
"A question of inspiration," *New Statesman and Nation,* 21 January 1950, p. 62 (article refuting implication of plagiarism).
"Little Flower Book," *Spectator,* CLXXXIV (30 June 1950), 879–80.
In Your Garden, Michael Joseph, London, 1951.
"Walter de la Mare and 'The Traveller,' " *Proceedings of the British Academy,* XXXIX (1953), 23–36 (Wharton Lecture on English poetry, 1953).
"The personality of Walter de la Mare," *Listener,* IL (30 April 1953), 711–2.
"Foreword" to Ernest Raymond, "The Brontë Legend: its cause and treatment," *Essays by Divers Hands,* N. S. XXVI (1953), Royal Society of Literature, London.
In Your Garden Again, Michael Joseph, London, 1953.
"Landscape of a mind," *Encounter,* II (January 1954) (article on Virginia Woolf).
"Censor for tiny tots," *Spectator,* CLII (5 February 1954), 152–3.
More For Your Garden, Michael Joseph, London, 1955.
"Virginia Woolf and Orlando," *Listener,* LIII (27 January 1955), 157–8.
"Green London," *Time and Tide,* 26 May 1956, p. 622.
"Little superstitions," *Listener,* LV (14 June 1956), 802–3.
"A child in the house," *Listener,* LVI (16 August 1956), 227–9.
Even More For Your Garden, Michael Joseph, London, 1958.
A Joy of Gardening: A selection for Americans, ed. Hermine Popper, Harper, New York, 1958.
Daughter of France, Michael Joseph, London, Doubleday, New York, 1959.
Faces: Profiles of dogs (with photographs by Laelia Goehr), Harvill Press, London, 1961, Doubleday, New York, 1962.

APPENDIX D

Survey of the Criticism

DURING HER LIFETIME V S-W attracted a good deal of attention as a novelist, a biographer, and a poet, in England, America, and on the Continent. Her books seem to have been reviewed by most of the important newspapers and literary magazines on both sides of the Atlantic, and were frequently also reviewed by continental newspapers, even when the book had not been translated.

In addition to reviews, some of them long and authoritative, several critical studies on her writing were published during her lifetime. The earliest of these were two which appeared in August 1923, one in England and one in America. They were followed six months later by another, published in England. As this was before V S-W had written any of the books for which she is chiefly remembered today, it seems to indicate that she was already regarded as a writer of some promise.

After the award of the Hawthornden Prize to *The Land* in June 1927, came a number of newspaper articles and interviews with V S-W. Few of them have much critical value, but they attest to a growing interest in her works among the public.

Immediately after the publication of *The Edwardians* in 1930, Hugh Walpole wrote a critical article about V S-W's writing in *Bookman,* New York, and this was followed the next year by another, signed J. S. Will in *Canadian Forum.* In December 1934 Mario Praz wrote about her prose in *La Stampa.* The next important article to appear was that written in 1940 by Richard Church. Originally it was published in the *Fortnightly Review,* but was reprinted later in *Eight for Immortality* a year later. This deals only with V S-W's poetry, as does the critical article by Jacques Vallette which appeared in *Mercure de France* in 1949, after the publication of *The Garden.* In between these comes a German essay by Hans Wagenseil which deals mainly with V S-W's prose works.

The best of the critical work, that by Richard Church and Jacques Vallette on her poetry, and by Mario Praz, Hans Wagenseil, and possibly Walpole on her prose, must be given serious consideration, as must critical remarks made by such well-known figures as Annette Kolb, as well as serious reviewers such as Raymond Mortimer, Augusto Guidi, Peter Quennell, and Desmond MacCarthy.

As regards V S-W and her public, there can be no doubt that she was and is read, and widely read. Several of her books have been reprinted many times: for example, from 1969 to 1971 *The Land* (1926), *The Edwardians* (1930), *All Passion Spent* (1931), *Saint Joan of Arc* (1936), *Pepita* (1937), *Daughter of France* (1959), and *No Signposts in the Sea* (1961) have all been reissued. It has proved impossible to find out exactly the number of copies of her books that have been sold, for the records of the Hogarth Press were lost during the war, and V S-W's American publisher, Doubleday and Co. Inc., refuse to release any figures, but as far as *The Edwardians* is concerned, it is possible to state that the sales were 30,000 copies for the first six months in England and 80,000 copies for the first year in America. It has been reprinted seventeen times in England, the German translation sold three editions (S. Fischer-Verlag, Berlin, 1931) in addition to which there was a Tauchnitz edition (Leipzig, 1931). The book has also been translated into Italian (Mondadori, Milan, 1952), French (Grasset, Paris, 1933), and Swedish (Bonniers, Stockholm, 1931).

The Land is now in its twenty-second edition and has sold, in England alone, approximately 100,000 copies.

During the first few years after V S-W's death no critical work on her was published. This is perfectly normal, and is accounted for partly by the fact that there is a lull in interest among the general public following the death of an author, and partly by the fact that those writers who intend to produce a serious critical study need several years in which to collect and collate their material before they are ready to start the actual writing. In V S-W's case the first study to appear was an unpublished master's thesis by Nancy Mac-Knight at Columbia University entitled "V. Sackville-West" (1968). In January 1972 came a published doctoral thesis, *V. Sackville-West: A Critical Biography,* by Michael Stevens, Stockholm, closely followed by Professor Sara Watson's *V. Sackville-West,* New York, 1972, and Nancy MacKnight's doctoral thesis, entitled "Vita: A Portrait of V. Sackville-West," Columbia University, 1972. It seems likely that others will appear in the near future; one, by Mme. Michel-Dalès, is now being written in Paris.

References

CHAPTER I

1   On her father's side . . . For this and other genealogical information in this
    chapter, see *Burke's Peerage and Baronetage,* London, 1970, pp. 2333–4. See also
    Harold Nicolson, *Diaries and Letters, 1945–62,* London, 1968, rear inside cover-
    papers, where a table of descent for V. Sackville-West's immediate ancestry is to
    be found; also V. Sackville-West, *Knole and the Sackvilles,* London, 1922, pp.
    ix–xii for a chronological table of the history of Knole and the Sackville family,
    and pp. xiv–xv for a simplified table of descent of the Sackvilles. Note that in
    this study, the edition of *Knole and the Sackvilles* used is that published by Benn,
    London, in 1958.
      For a detailed description of the Sackville family and its descent, see Phil-
    lips, *The history of the Sackville family, together with a description of Knole and the early
    owners of Knole,* London, 1930, Vols. I and II.

1   On her mother's side . . . See Nicolson, *op. cit.,* inside rear cover-papers; *Dic-
    tionary of National Biography,* 2nd Supplement, London, 1912, p. 249; V. Sack-
    ville-West, *Pepita,* Hogarth Press, London, 1937, pp. 52ff.

1   "There Sackville's sonnets . . ." Quoted in *Knole and the Sackvilles,* p. 44.

1   At the age of thirty . . . Paul Bacquet, *Un contemporain d'Elisabeth I, Thomas Sack-
    ville,* Genève, 1966, is probably the leading work on Thomas Sackville. For de-
    tails of the relationship between him and Queen Elizabeth, see p. 15. See also
    Phillips, *op. cit.,* I, 187, and *Knole and the Sackvilles,* p. 46.

1   and, in 1599 . . . *Burke's Peerage and Baronetage* appears to be wrong here. This
    work gives the date as 1594 (p. 2333). *Knole and the Sackvilles* gives 1599 (p. 46),
    as do Bacquet, *op. cit.,* p. 78 and Phillips, *op. cit.,* I, 211, both of which quote Cal.
    State Pap. (Dom.), Vol. CCLXX (15 May 1599), 194 as their authority.

2   Pepita left Spain . . . For further details, see the review of *Pepita* by Gustaf
    Stridsberg in *Svenska Dagbladet,* 13 November 1938, p. 8.

6   *persona non grata* Phillips, *op. cit.,* II, pp. 325–6, and *Pepita,* pp. 167–72. An inter-
    esting inquiry into the identity of the true author of the Murchison letter and

the political situation which rendered it such an effective campaign weapon is the article by T. C. Hinckely, "George Osgoodby and the Murchison Letter," Biographical footnotes, *Pacific Historical Review*, Univ. of California Press, Berkeley, XXVII (November 1958), 359–70.

The justification, or rather, lack of justification for the American Secretary of State's action in handing Lionel Sackville-West back his passport is discussed at some length in an illuminating article, "The Dismissal of Lord Sackville," C. S. Campbell, Jr., Biographical footnotes, *Mississippi Valley Historical Review*, XLIV (March 1958), 635–48.

CHAPTER II

7   "the best type . . ." *Pepita*, p. 237.

7   "My mother was . . ." *Ibid.*, p. 201.

8   "Many people have . . ." *Ibid.*, p. 282.

8   One of the people . . . An excellent character-sketch of Sir John Murray Scott together with some details of his life is to be found in *Pepita*, pp. 189–200.

8   Sir John seems . . . *Pepita*, p. 190. According to V S-W, the evening Sir John met her, "he added a codicil to his will by which he left her the sum of £ 50,000."

10   a blaze of publicity . . . The case "Sackville-West v. West, Attorney General and others" was reported in some detail on page 3 of *The Times* on the 2nd, 3rd, 5th, 9th, 15th, and 26th of February, 1910. It was frontpage news on these dates in the more sensational press.

10   Henri's case collapsed . . . *Pepita*, pp. 211–29. When Lord and Lady Sackville reached Sevenoaks, the fire brigade took the horses out of the shafts of the victoria and drew the carriage by hand through the streets of the town right into the courtyard of Knole.

10   after a brilliant defense . . . *Pepita*, pp. 242–6. The case "Capron v. Scott" was reported very fully in *The Times*, 17 June 1913, p. 3; 25 June, pp. 5, 8; 27 June, p. 67; and page 5 on 28 June, 1 July, 2 July, 4 July, 5 July, 8 July.

11   "She loved me . . ." MS Autobiography, p. 12.

11   "I can't remember . . ." *Ibid.*, p. 2.

11   "she says she would . . ." *Ibid.*, p. 12.

11   "very old, and queer . . ." *Ibid.*, p. 3.

11   "Of all human beings . . ." *Ibid.*, p. 6.

12   "always grubby and . . ." *Ibid.*, p. 10.

12   "The drawing of Vita's . . ." Lady Sackville's Diary, 20 February 1903.

12   "Vita and I went . . ." *Ibid.*, 17 August 1906.

13   "Such a man . . ." *Pepita*, pp. 237–8.

13   "I think that . . ." MS Autobiography, pp. 17–18.

13   "I set myself . . ." *Ibid.*, p. 18.

14   "I wasn't hated . . ." *Ibid.*, p. 19.

14   quite capable of spending . . . *Pepita*, p. 246.

PAGE

14 *"Regarde, comme ce . . ."* *Ibid.,* p. 206. ("See how much better this paper is for writing on than Bromo.")

14 "I remember very . . ." MS Autobiography, p. 3.

14 "There certainly *was* . . ." *Ibid.,* p. 5.

15 The reason why . . . Eloquent testimony to the strength of her personality was given by the celebrated F. E. Smith, during the lawsuit over Sir John's will: "He asked the jury whether, in all their acquaintance with the courts, they ever saw a lady of a more arresting and dominating personality . . . than Lady Sackville? The jury had seen in the witness-box one of the strongest and most striking personalities they had met in their lives." *Daily Chronicle,* 8 July 1913, p. 5.

15 "I wanted to take . . ." Lady Sackville's Diary, 2 June 1910.

15 "How my mother . . ." *Pepita,* p. 206.

17 "Of course she . . ." *Ibid.,* pp. 232–3. ("Just look at that old horror over there, my dear: doesn't she look frightful in that wig? How can people rig themselves up like that!")

18 "She was surrounded . . ." *Pepita,* p. 181.

18 "I know I was . . ." MS Autobiography, p. 3.

19 "Leonard Antequil . . ." *The Edwardians,* pp. 12–15. Note that in this study, the edition of *The Edwardians* used is that published by Arrow Books Ltd., London, 1960.

19 "I forgot to say . . ." MS Autobiography, p. 10.

20 "a trait I inherit . . ." MS Autobiography, p. 10.

20 "Knole is not . . ." *Knole and the Sackvilles,* pp. 28–9.

21 "You know me . . ." *Diaries and Letters, 1945–62,* p. 322.

21 "How much I prefer . . ." *Diaries and Letters, 1939–45,* p. 472.

21 "There are times . . ." MS in the possession of Nigel Nicolson, Sissinghurst Castle. See also the poem, "I suppose other people endure the same dissatisfactions," on p. 152 above.

22 "Took Vita with . . ." This entry, for February 25, 1903, refers to Charles Sackville-West, later 4th Baron Sackville, V S-W's uncle, and her cousin, Edward Sackville-West, later 5th Baron Sackville.

22 "Oh Hadji . . ." *Diaries and Letters, 1945–62,* p. 196.

23 "When I was about . . ." MS Autobiography, p. 17.

23 her first novel . . . "Edward Sackville, Earl of Dorset."

23 The following year . . . The MSS of all these plays and novels are at Sissinghurst Castle.

23 " £1. I had . . ." V S-W's diary, 12 July 1907.

23 "we only really knew . . ." *Diaries and Letters, 1930–39,* p. 16.

23 "I have finished . . ." Lady Sackville's diary, 16 October 1907.

24 *"Mistress Chatterton. . . ."* *Chatterton* I:4.

25 *"Archer. . . ."* *Ibid.,* I:6.

25 *"Chatterton. . . ."* *Ibid.,* I:5.

25 "How much I loved . . ." MS Autobiography, p. 24.

PAGE

26 "The first remark . . ." *Ibid.,* p. 24.

26 "Mother, who doesn't . . ." *Ibid.,* p. 34.

CHAPTER III

28 "Harold far more . . ." MS Autobiography, p. 30.

28 "He was as gay . . ." *Ibid.,* p. 27.

28 "I remember a . . ." *Ibid.,* p. 36.

29 "That was the . . ." *Ibid.*

29 *Poems of West and East.* Of the twenty-two poems in this volume, one, "The Dancing Elf," had been published in the *English Review* in August 1913, and eight poems published privately in *Constantinople,* 1915.

30 "my liaison with Rosamund . . ." MS Autobiography, p. 27.

32 The aftereffects . . . Later on V S-W's affairs became quite well-known in certain circles. In the late 'twenties the South African poet Roy Campbell, furious because his wife had fallen in love with V S-W, wrote a long satirical poem in imitation of the *Dunciad* ridiculing the Nicolsons and Georgian poets. It contains, among other things, the following passage:

> Now fully armed the direct foe to meet,
> This new 'Orlando' flounces to his feet,
> And with a virginally vulpine air,
> The hair-pins falling from his frowsy hair,
> First meets his own approval in the glass,
> Then tries his voice, to see if it will pass,
> And finds the organ, beat it if you can,
> Able to lisp as sweetly as a man,
> Or roll far down into as deep a bass
> As any lady-writer in the place.
> It was a voice of 1930 model
> And in a Bloomsbury accent it could yodel
> Between its tonsils drawling out long O's
> Along its draughty, supercilious nose.
> "The Georgiad," *Collected Poems* Vol. I,
> London, 1949, p. 203.

By this time it was a fairly open secret that the hero/heroine of Virginia Woolf's *Orlando* was a portrait of V S-W.

32 The most immediate result . . . It is this autobiography that *Portrait of a Marriage* is based on. In 1970, while writing this book, I had the privilege of reading it, although at that time only a few details could be used as Violet Trefusis was still alive.

33 *King's Daughter* . . . Violet Trefusis was not King Edward VII's daughter. She was born in 1894, and according to Philip Magnus (*King Edward the Seventh,* London, 1964, p. 260) the relationship between Alice Keppel and Edward did not begin until February 1898. It would nevertheless have been quite in keeping with her beliefs about her own ancestry if V S-W had imagined Violet to be Edward's daughter—until she wrote Pepita in 1936 she had thought that Pepita was the illegitimate daughter of the Duke of Osuna.

PAGE

33 "it accounts for . . ." MS Autobiography, p. 7.

34 "in the subsequent . . ." *Heritage,* Collins, London, 1919, pp. 42–3.

34 "He cringes to . . ." *Ibid.,* p. 60.

34 "Ruth loved me . . ." *Ibid.,* pp. 236–7.

34 in several of her books . . . They are: *Heritage,* 1919, *The Dragon in Shallow Waters,* 1921, *Grey Wethers,* 1923, *The Land,* 1926, *The Death of Noble Godavary,* 1932, and *Pepita,* 1937.

36 "The upper half . . ." MS Autobiography, p. 31.

36 "What has always . . ." *Diaries and Letters, 1939–45,* p. 157.

36 "Luckily for you . . ." *Ibid.,* p. 266.

36 "a queer tale . . ." *Times Literary Supplement,* 16 June 1921, p. 386.

37 "ruthless savagery . . ." *The Dragon in Shallow Waters,* Collins, London, p. 107.

37 "really rather depressed . . ." *Diaries and Letters, 1945–62,* p. 183.

37 "Darling, I must write . . ." *Ibid.,* pp. 195–6.

38 "Elle a écrit . . ." "Victoria Sackville-West," *Mercure de France,* 1-III-1949, pp. 423–4. ("In prose she has written the lives of some saints, the story of her Spanish grandmother (*Pepita*), a novel (*The Edwardians*), some long short-stories (*All Passion Spent*). But she thinks of herself as a poet above all and wishes to be judged by a collection of verse written between 1913 and the Second World War, to which was added in 1946 a second sequence, *The Garden.*")

38 "Poetry every time . . ." *Everyman,* 23 October 1930, p. 392.

40 "the one fabulous . . ." *The Heir,* Heinemann, London, 1922, p. 247.

40 "the parrot no longer . . ." *Ibid.,* pp. 248–9.

40 two-volume history of the house and family. Charles J. Phillips, *History of the Sackville family, together with a description of Knole and the early owners of Knole,* Cassel, London, 1930.

41 "I've done my proofs . . ." *Diaries and Letters, 1945–1962,* p. 110.

41 "like a lover to her," . . . *Diaries and Letters, 1930–1939,* p. 17.

41 "Knole, when I went from you, . . ." For the full text of the poem, see p. 149 above.

41 "I should never . . ." Unpublished letter dated 3 January 1923, in the possession of Nigel Nicolson.

41 Eddie's Georgians . . . *Georgian Poetry,* ed. Edward Marsh, London, 1922.

42 A brief life . . . A description of Lady Anne's life together with extracts from her diary and other writings by her will be found in Phillips, *op. cit.,* I, 276–88. See also the *Complete Peerage,* III (1913), 295–7, and *D.N.B.,* XI (1887), 56–7.

42 "stands as instance . . ." *Spectator,* CXXXI (11 August 1923), 197.

42 ". . . an enchanted village . . ." *Times Literary Supplement,* 23 June 1923, p. 438.

42 a debt to *Wuthering Heights* . . . The only two pictures in V S-W's study, apart from family photographs, were a portrait of Virginia Woolf and a reproduction of Branwell Brontë's painting of his sisters.

43 "He was the darkness . . ." *Grey Wethers,* Heinemann, London, p. 280.

43 This is stressed . . . *Ibid.,* p. 81: "In essence, they were equal; different of

PAGE

course, he male, she female, but united they made a whole, each contributing an equal share."

43 In Calladine, V S-W . . . *Grey Wethers* was probably the first novel she wrote after the crisis of 1920. These passages seem to indicate how serious the crisis was, and how long the aftereffects lasted. See also V S-W's remarks on her character quoted on pp. 36–37 above.

43 "He was a believer . . ." *Ibid.,* p. 198.

43 "appeared satisfied, . . ." *Ibid.,* p. 201.

43 "Always looking out . . ." *Ibid.,* p. 263.

43 "had before him . . ." *Ibid.,* p. 100.

43 "And then I came . . ." *The Land,* William Heinemann, London, 1926, pp. 49–50.

44 Julian and Eve . . . Nigel Nicolson says on p. 148 of *Portrait of a Marriage* that *Challenge* is dedicated to Violet. So it is in fact, but not in word, the dedication being: ACABA EMBEO SIN TIRO, MEN CHUAJAÑI; LIRENAS, BERJARAS TIRI OCHI BUSÑE, CHANGERI, TA ARMENSALLE.—which is Spanish Romany for "This book is for you, my dear witch; the noble ones would have read it and considered your soul false, but free." V S-W spoke no Spanish Romany, but must have looked up the individual words in a dictionary, clearly some time after 1920.

44 "a novel of . . ." *New York Times,* Book Review, 18 February 1923, p. 11.

46 "It is not, . . ." Pippett, *The Moth and the Star,* Boston, 1955, p. 173.

46 "What the tale . . ." *Times Literary Supplement,* 27 November 1924, p. 794.

46 "with a rapidity . . ." *Seducers in Ecuador,* Hogarth Press, London, 1924, p. 10.

46 "since Robert existed, . . ." *Ibid.,* p. 51.

47 "Lomax at night . . ." *Ibid.,* p. 68.

47 During her nearly . . . *Passenger to Teheran,* Hogarth Press, London, 1926, pp. 107–37.

48 "But in the meantime . . ." *Ibid.,* p. 100.

48 "There must . . ." *Ibid.,* p. 123.

48 "The contrast was . . ." *Twelve Days,* Hogarth Press, London, 1928, pp. 121–2.

49 "I write as one . . ." *Ibid.,* pp. 80–1.

49 in the oral tradition . . . Although V S-W experienced difficulty in establishing contact with people (see above, p. 21), this did not apply to her relationship with servants, etc., as her article entitled "The Edwardians Below Stairs," *Vogue,* 25 November 1931, pp. 55–7, shows. She would have had no difficulty in discussing agriculture with farmers.

49 "the truth it tells . . ." *Times Literary Supplement,* 30 November 1933, p. 852.

49 "*The Land* is . . ." "V. Sackville-West: A Poet in a Tradition," *Fortnightly Review,* CXLVIII (1940), 603.

50 "All craftsmen share . . ." *The Land,* p. 81.

50 "*My Manifesto:* . . ." *Diaries and Letters, 1939–45,* p. 433.

51 "Brother to all . . ." *The Land,* p. 80.

51 "Be prouder than . . ." *Ibid.,* p. 72.

PAGE

51 "It's my boy, . . ." *The Edwardians*, pp. 40–1.

52 Aphra Behn's early life . . . H. D. Benjamin, "Een Koninklijke slaav in Suriname," *De West-Indische Gids*, Amsterdam, October 1919; "Nog eens: Aphra Behn," *Ibid.*, February 1921; "Is Aphra Behn in Suriname geweest?," *Ibid.*, February 1927.

52 "that Mrs. Behn . . ." *Aphra Behn*, Gerald Howe, London, 1927, p. 72.

52 "the fact that . . ." *Ibid.*, p. 12.

52 Dr. Bernbaum had made . . . Ernest Bernbaum, "Mrs. Behn's Biography a Fiction," *Kittredge Anniversary Papers*, 1913. In *Aphra Behn* (p. 21), V S-W writes: "But now comes Dr. Bernbaum and says that none of this is true. Mrs. Behn, he says, never went to Surinam at all. She never saw a marble palace floating on the English Channel, therefore she never saw Surinam. Her father, he says, was not her father, nor was he ever appointed Governor of Surinam or any other colony. She never knew Oroonoko; never came within measurable distance of him. If she could lie about Prince Tarquin, she could lie about Oroonoko. Was his name, indeed, Oroonoko? Was she not thinking of the winding river called Orinoco, whose Indian significance is 'coiled serpent'? Was her own name, indeed, Mrs. Behn? Was there ever a Mr. Behn? What proof have we of his existence? Gildon says there was a Mr. Behn, but then Gildon was a liar. . . . Dr. Bernbaum . . . goes (on) to prove that the *Life and Memoirs* was full of false biographical detail, and moreover was not written by one 'of the fair sex' but by Gildon himself."

52 "In the evening . . ." *Diaries and Letters, 1945–62*, pp. 385–6.

53 "This, as always, . . ." *Ibid.*, p. 71.

53 "I will hold to . . ." MS in the possession of Nigel Nicolson. For the full text of the poem see pp. 150–51 below.

53 "I go . . ." *Diaries and Letters, 1945–62*, p. 72.

55 "something wilder and . . ." Virginia Woolf, *A Writer's Diary*, London, 1954, p. 79.

55 "I am writing *Orlando* . . ." *Ibid.*, p. 117.

55 Violet Trefusis as the Princess . . . *Orlando*, pp. 48–50.

55 Nigel Nicolson and Joanne Trautmann . . . *Portrait of a Marriage*, Atheneum, New York, 1973, and *The Jessamy Brides: The Friendship of Virginia Woolf and V. Sackville-West*, Penn State Studies, 1973.

55 "Orlando and her husband . . ." *Feminism and Art*, University of Chicago Press, Chicago, 1968, pp. 115–16.

55 "she [Orlando] was censuring . . ." *Orlando*, p. 145.

57 "The mentally androgynous . . ." *The Glass Roof: Virginia Woolf as Novelist*, University of California Press, Berkeley, 1954, p. 104.

57 "Each was perfectly . . ." See Nigel Nicolson, *Portrait of a Marriage*, pp. 136–8, 187–8.

57 "was open to . . ." *Andrew Marvell*, Faber & Faber, London, 1929, pp. 32–3.

57 "To Marvell . . ." *Ibid.*, pp. 33–4.

58 "it was not to be expected . . ." *Ibid.*, p. 27.

58 "What worries me . . ." *Diaries and Letters, 1945–62*, p. 38.

PAGE

58 By 1927 . . . *Sweet Waters*, Constable, London, 1921; *Paul Verlaine*, Constable, London, 1921; *Tennyson*, Constable, 1923; *Byron: The Last Journey*, Constable, 1924; *Swinburne*, Macmillan, London, 1927; *Some People*, Constable, 1927; *The Development of English Biography*, Hogarth Press, London, 1927.

59 "What is so . . ." *Diaries and Letters, 1930–39*, pp. 33–4.

CHAPTER IV

61 "Vita telephones to . . ." *Diaries and Letters, 1930–39*, p. 44.

61 "a house in ruins . . ." *Ibid.*, pp. 43, 425.

62 "My view is: . . ." *Ibid.*, pp. 47–8.

63 "Through its veins . . ." *Ibid.*, p. 47.

65 "As the thousands . . ." *Downhill All the Way*, Hogarth Press, London, p. 113.

65 "a tired swimmer . . ." This and the following quotations are all from the first 64 lines of "Sissinghurst," Hogarth Press, London, 1931. Reprinted in *Collected Poems*, Hogarth Press, London, 1933, pp. 111–4.

66 "H. said that . . ." *Diaries and Letters, 1945–62*, p. 268.

66 "how fortunate we . . ." *Ibid.*, p. 183.

66 "a novel about Knole . . ." *Downhill All the Way*, p. 158.

67 "Quite apart from . . ." *Daily Telegraph*, May 1930.

67 the artificiality and uselessness . . . Anita Leslie, the granddaughter of Leonie Jerome, whose sister, Jennie Jerome Churchill, was Winston Churchill's mother, says in her book *The Marlborough House Set* (p. 309): "Several of the personages of this book have been depicted under other names in V. Sackville-West's novel *The Edwardians*, a volume which caused some consternation among living Edwardians when it was first published in 1930."

67 "I will agree . . ." *The Edwardians*, p. 182.

67 "Very well, if . . ." *Ibid.*, pp. 121–2.

68 "We published . . ." *Downhill All the Way*, p. 159.

69 "a study of extreme . . ." *New Statesman and Nation*, I (6 June 1931), 547.

69 "the study of a contemplative . . ." *Manchester Guardian*, 2 June 1931, p. 11.

69 "even had she . . ." *All Passion Spent*, pp. 160–1.

70 A brief account . . . *Diaries and Letters, 1930–39*, pp. 218–25.

71 "They looked as though . . ." *Family History*, Hogarth Press, London, 1932, p. 53.

71 "believe in reputation . . ." *Ibid.*, p. 141.

71 "She begins with . . ." *New Statesman and Nation*, IV (22 October 1932), 490.

71 "there are moments . . ." *New York Times*, Book Review, 30 October 1932, p. 7.

72 "As to remembering . . ." *Diaries and Letters, 1939–45*, pp. 447–8. The lines are from Dryden, *All for Love*, IV.i.

72 "The discovery led . . ." *New Statesman and Nation*, 21 January 1950, p. 62. A copy of the article will be found in Appendix A, on pp. 145–148 above.

PAGE

73 "I think it is . . ." *Diaries and Letters, 1930–39,* p. 136.

73 "with all their kindness . . ." *Ibid.,* p. 136.

73 "Earth and not pavement . . ." "In New England," *Collected Poems,* London, 1933, p. 212.

73 one which she never published. "Minnesota," MS at Sissinghurst Castle.

74 "The Driscolls' house . . ." *Grand Canyon,* Michael Joseph, London, 1942, pp. 20–1.

74 "this collection of poems . . ." *New Statesman and Nation,* VII (12 May 1934), 740.

75 "*The Dark Island, . . .*" *Times Literary Supplement,* 11 October 1934, p. 692.

75 The *New York Times* . . . Book Review, 25 November 1934, p. 6.

75 The *Manchester Guardian.* 2 November 1934.

75 The *New Statesman and Nation* . . . VIII (1 December 1934), 794.

75 "grave doubts . . ." *Downhill All the Way,* p. 159.

75 "Darling, I am . . ." *Diaries and Letters, 1930–39,* pp. 185–6.

76 "There was a curious . . ." *Downhill All the Way,* p. 112.

76 "Vita was in many ways . . ." *The Journey Not the Arrival Matters,* Hogarth Press, London, 1969, p. 57.

76 Shirin is a slightly . . . This was confirmed by Nigel Nicolson in a letter of 13 January 1971.

77 Storn, the dark island . . . The name "Storn" was possibly suggested to V S-W by the name of Lord Beaverbrook's home, Stornoway House, which H.N. had recently visited several times.

77 "with a cold and . . ." *The Dark Island,* Hogarth Press, London, 1934, p. 179.

77 "Already at sixteen . . ." *Ibid.,* pp. 32–3.

78 in the game of "It" . . . *Ibid.,* pp. 198–202, 217.

78 gives Shirin a massage . . . *Ibid.,* pp. 84–94.

79 "In January 1936, . . ." *Diaries and Letters, 1930–39,* p. 28.

79 "Patience, intuition . . ." *Times Literary Supplement,* 6 June 1936, p. 469.

80 *The Eagle and the Dove* . . . Michael Joseph, London. In this study, the Mermaid Book edition, Michael Joseph, London, 1953, has been used throughout.

80 "not what is called . . ." *Saint Joan of Arc,* Cobden, Sanderson, London, 1936, p. 382. In this study, the edition by Penguin Books, London, 1955, has been used throughout.

80 "in the unfortunate . . ." *Ibid.,* p. 383.

81 in the *Observer* . . . 7 November 1937, p. 11.

81 the *New Statesman and Nation* . . . XIV (30 October 1937), 695.

81 "she brought us . . ." *Downhill All the Way,* pp. 159–60.

81 The novel was . . . This was confirmed in a letter dated 1 January 1971 from Nigel Nicolson.

81 V S-W was feeling . . . *Diaries and Letters, 1939–45,* pp. 156–7.

82 she and Gwen St. Aubyn . . . *Diaries and Letters, 1930–39,* p. 311.

PAGE

83   "So, rightly, you . . ." *Solitude,* Hogarth Press, London, p. 5.

84   "—but who would sleep . . ." *Ibid.,* p. 7.

84   "—but who would wake . . ." *Ibid.,* p. 56.

84   "Hurry on! . . ." *Ibid.,* p. 37.

84   "And since I . . ." *Ibid.,* p. 20.

84   "No Church I . . ." *Ibid.,* p. 21.

85   "Give us a . . ." *Ibid.,* p. 46.

85   "But silence . . ." *Ibid.,* p. 51.

85   ". . . that happy, . . ." *Ibid.,* p. 48.

85   "We only ask . . ." *Ibid.,* p. 46.

86   a Lesbian relationship . . . *The Eagle and the Dove,* p. 28.

86   "one of the most . . ." *Ibid.,* p. 68.

86   "the reader who . . ." *Ibid.,* p. 69.

86   "in addition to . . ." *Ibid.,* p. 60.

86   "The mystics . . ." *Ibid.,* p. 44.

86   "We may well . . ." *Ibid.,* pp. 43–4.

87   "for there is . . ." *Ibid.,* p. 146.

87   *Diaries and Letters, 1930–39* . . . P. 311.

87   "under war-time . . ." *The Eagle and the Dove,* p. 7.

87   In an article . . . "Question of Inspiration," *New Statesman and Nation,* 21 January 1950, p. 62. The article is reprinted in Appendix A above.

87   "a recently converted . . ." *Loc. cit.*

88   "The roaring of . . ." *The Eagle and the Dove,* p. 183.

89   "Oh Days, be . . ." *The Garden,* p. 128.

89   "the horrible loneliness . . ." Quotation from the unpublished poem to be found on p. 152 above.

89   "For our life . . ." *The Garden,* p. 103.

89   "Truths surrounded . . ." *Ibid.,* p. 44.

90   "—Christ would have . . ." *Ibid.,* p. 49.

90   "Then in the poignant . . ." *Ibid.,* pp. 70–1.

90   "There is another . . ." *Ibid.,* p. 89.

91   "Halt, and consider . . ." *Ibid.,* p. 128.

91   "I had not . . ." The MS is undated, but was found in December 1963 lying last in a file marked "Mostly 1940 to 1945." The file had almost certainly not been looked at since V S-W's death.

CHAPTER V

96   "I'm no criminal . . ." *Devil at Westease,* Doubleday, New York, 1947, p. 192.

96   "The solution is . . ." *New York Times,* Book Review, 11 May 1947, p. 31.

96   "she isn't *quite* . . ." *Diaries and Letters, 1945–62,* p. 88.

PAGE

96 "Her own description . . ." *Ibid.*, p. 88.

97 "Companion of Honour . . ." See the citation in *The Times*, 1 January 1948, p. 6.

97 "Now supposing Pepita . . ." *Diaries and Letters, 1945–62*, p. 164.

98 "I am really . . ." *Ibid.*, pp. 183–4.

98 "Darling, I must . . ." *Ibid.*, p. 195.

98 "After such triumphs . . ." *Observer*, 25 January 1953.

99 "My poor Viti . . ." *Diaries and Letters, 1945–62*, p. 236.

99 "It hinges on . . ." *Times Literary Supplement*, 6 February 1953, p. 88.

100 "a sense of the . . ." *The Easter Party*, Michael Joseph, London, pp. 49–50.

100 "I want my marriage . . ." *Ibid.*, p. 55.

100 "I can at least . . ." *Ibid.*

100 "his chosen celibacy" . . . *Ibid.*, p. 95.

100 "There was something . . ." *Ibid.*, p. 70.

101 "her pantheism . . ." *Ibid.*, pp. 97–8.

101 The strange incident . . . *Ibid.*, pp. 88–9.

101 and its sequel . . . *Ibid.*, p. 94.

101 "Walter darling, . . ." *Ibid.*, p. 81.

101 "there are only two . . ." *Ibid.*, p. 120.

101 "Svend . . ." Svend is based on V S-W's Alsatian, Rollo.

101 Throughout the book . . . *Ibid.*, pp. 96, 100, 103, 113.

101 "You are both . . ." *Ibid.*, p. 121.

101 "for once, Walter . . ." *Ibid.*, p. 160.

101 "he seemed transformed, . . ." *Ibid.*, p. 165.

102 "I revive the idea . . ." *Diaries and Letters, 1945–62*, p. 237.

102 She struggled on . . . *Ibid.*, p. 255.

102 "The Big Miss . . ." *Ibid.*

102 "Francis Steegmuller . . ." *La Grande Mademoiselle*, Hamish Hamilton, London, 1955.

102 "V. has written . . ." Harold Nicolson, *Journey to Java*, Constable, London, 1957, p. 218.

103 "Do you know . . ." *Diaries and Letters, 1945–62*, p. 351.

103 "Her story is to be . . ." *Times Literary Supplement*, 8 May 1959, p. 267.

103 "Le Grand Siècle . . ." *Diaries and Letters, 1945–62*, p. 88.

104 "It is primarily . . ." *Observer*, 5 April 1959, p. 21.

104 "her clear-sighted . . ." *Times Literary Supplement*, 8 May 1959, p. 267.

104 "the simple, touching . . ." *Ibid.*

105 "Years ago, in . . ." *Times Literary Supplement*, 10 February 1961, p. 85.

105 "I have never known . . ." *No Signposts in the Sea*, Michael Joseph, London, 1961, p. 35.

105 "I knew two . . ." *Ibid.*, p. 136.

PAGE

107   For her, the essentials . . . *Ibid.*, p. 87.

107   "There is nothing . . ." *Ibid.*, p. 89.

107   "Let there be . . ." *Ibid.*, p. 90. The quotation is taken from *The Prophet* by Kahlil Gibran, London, 1926, p. 15.

108   "Apparently they had . . ." *Ibid.*, p. 48.

108   "I wish that . . ." *Ibid.*, p. 146.

108   "He is genuine . . ." *Ibid.*, p. 82.

108   "by no means . . ." *Ibid.*, p. 25.

108   "the out-of-the-way . . ." *Ibid.*, p. 32.

108   In several places . . . *Ibid.*, pp. 25, 55, and 77.

108   "a touch of . . ." *Ibid.*, p. 32.

108   "can't stand . . ." *Ibid.*, p. 54.

109   "so unmistakably English. . . ." *Ibid.*, p. 78.

109   The ideal portrait . . . See above, p. 7.

109   a long short-story . . . "Interlude in Two Lives," *Woman's Own,* 24 and 30 March 1962.

109   "*Disastrous* journey. . . ." *Diaries and Letters, 1945–62,* p. 406.

CHAPTER VI

110   "nor had she . . ." *Diaries and Letters, 1930–39,* p. 18.

110   Her difficulty in . . . See above, p. 21, and the unpublished poem, above, p. 152.

110   As she points out . . . *No Signposts in the Sea,* pp. 87, 133–4.

110   "I thought how . . ." *Diaries and Letters, 1945–62,* p. 386.

111   This appears to be . . . Two of the periods in which V S-W wrote fiction are clearly defined: 1919–24 and 1930–34. During the third, 1942–61, novels appeared at irregular intervals.

111   These were the years . . . See above, p. 30.

111   In this somber book, . . . See above, pp. 75–78.

111   the character of exorcism . . . *Pepita,* written after the end of her mother's influence over her, and *Devil at Westease,* which seems to mark the end of her concern with duality. See above, pp. 95–96.

112   "Every novel written . . ." *Spectator,* 6 February 1953, p. 158.

113   The phrase which gives . . . *No Signposts in the Sea,* p. 28.

113   "there are no tombstones . . ." *Ibid.*, p. 48.

113   the "man overboard . . ." *Ibid.*, pp. 47–8.

113   Edmund Carr's burial . . . *Ibid.*, p. 156.

113   This poem, the whole . . . See above, pp. 83–85.

113   In *The Garden,* . . . See Stevens, *op. cit.,* pp. 41–53.

113   She could never . . . During the early 'twenties she did, however, show some of

PAGE

her poetry to Edward Marsh before publishing it, as her correspondence with him shows. See Christopher Hassall, *Edward Marsh: A Biography*, London, 1959, pp. 513–14.

113   "I can't even mention . . ." *Everyman*, 23 October 1930, p. 392. Other authors have said much the same thing; for example, Somerset Maugham in the "Author's Preface" to *Cakes and Ale*.

116   Lowell complains . . . *New York Times*, Book Review, March 26, 1922.

117   an American researcher . . . Joanne Trautmann, *The Jessamy Brides: The Friendship of Virginia Woolf and V. Sackville-West*, Penn State Studies, 1973, pp. 29–30.

CHAPTER VII

118   "to a certain . . ." *The Development of English Biography*, Hogarth Press, 1927, p. 10.

119   the article on George Eliot . . . Ed. H. J. and H. Massingham, *The Great Victorians*, London, 1932, pp. 187–95.

119   "claimed equal rights . . ." *Aphra Behn*, p. 13.

119   "then descend to . . ." *Ibid.*, p. 74.

119   "And as she . . ." *Ibid.*, p. 77.

120   "Is that poetry? . . ." *Ibid.*, p. 84.

120   "the most original . . ." *Ibid.*, p. 74.

120   "The songs are . . ." *Ibid.*, p. 84.

120   "Indeed, this whole, . . ." *Ibid.*

120   calling herself Mary Marvell . . . Mary Palmer edited Marvell's poems as "the exact copies of my late dear husband, under his own handwriting, being found since his death among his papers," probably in an attempt to substantiate her claim to be his widow so that she might lay her hands on £ 500 which he had been taking care of for two bankrupt friends. V S-W did not know about Mary Palmer, but suspected that she was either a fraud, or existed only in the shrewd publisher's imagination. "In the whole of Marvell's own correspondence, as in all contemporary writing concerning him, there is no mention whatsoever of a wife; on the contrary, such allusions as were made to his private life, pointed to quite different conclusions" (*Andrew Marvell*, p. 23). V S-W does not state what conclusions they do point to.

121   misleading body of criticism . . . Those interested are invited to consult the Penguin Critical Anthology, *Andrew Marvell*, ed. John Carey, London, 1969.

121   "that sense of man's . . ." V S-W, *Andrew Marvell*, p. 34.

121   "his was a dual . . ." *Ibid.*, p. 61.

122   *Another World Than This* . . . Pp. 80, 146.

122   "wonder what her . . ." *The Great Victorians*, p. 191.

122   "Without going so far . . ." *Ibid.*, p. 188.

122   "She was no flaming . . ." *Ibid.*, p. 189.

122   "Unfortunately . . . George Eliot . . ." *Ibid.*, p. 193.

PAGE

123 "She let herself . . ." *The Great Victorians,* p. 194.

123 ". . . over Tito . . ." Tito Melema, the male character in *Romola,* described by Sir Leslie Stephen in his article on George Eliot (*Dictionary of National Biography*) as "thoroughly and to his fingers' ends a woman."

123 "We may presume . . ." *Saint Joan of Arc,* p. 14.

123 "I think it is not . . ." *Ibid.,* pp. 17–18.

123 "a serious and . . ." *Ibid.,* p. 37.

123 "browbeating a king . . ." *Ibid.,* p. 22.

123 "She was, in fact, . . ." *Ibid.,* p. 23.

124 "was a woman . . ." *Ibid.,* p. 30.

124 "as Charles VII . . ." *Ibid.,* p. 132.

125 *Portrait of a Marriage* . . . P. 53.

125 *Diaries and Letters* . . . Vol. I (1930–1939), pp. 34, 109, 148, 153, 158, 159.

125 "the duality of her . . ." *The Eagle and the Dove,* p. 71.

126 "the Velasquez or . . ." *Ibid.,* p. 139.

126 "In secular life . . ." *Ibid.,* pp. 124, 125.

126 "Never to fail . . ." *Ibid.,* p. 138.

126 "It must be admitted . . ." *Ibid.,* p. 154.

127 "It would be a shallow . . ." *Ibid.,* p. 160.

127 "there was a touch . . ." *Daughter of France,* p. 143.

128 "She lay in state . . ." Louis de Rouvroy, duc de St. Simon, quoted in *Daughter of France,* p. 335.

128 "She had not been . . ." *Daughter of France,* p. 173.

129 discussing the complicated state . . . "It would be wearisome to go into details of what she financially gained by his death, and as I can never understand my own finances in 1959, I don't see why I should be expected to understand Mademoiselle's in 1660, nearly three hundred years ago."

CHAPTER VIII

131 "For some years . . ." Robert H. Ross, *The Georgian Revolt: Rise and Fall of a Poetic Ideal, 1910–1922,* Southern Illinois University Press, 1965. p. ix.

131 "a part of the larger . . ." *Ibid.,* p. 22.

132 "affected and self-conscious . . ." *Times Literary Supplement,* 27 February 1913, p. 81.

132 "The Neo-Georgians were . . ." Ross, *op. cit.,* p. 165.

132 seven poems . . . They were: "A Saxon Song," "Mariana in the North," "Full Moon," "Sailing Ships," "Trio," "Bitterness," and "Evening."

132 As Ross says . . . Ross, *op. cit.,* p. 212.

133 "She was wearing . . ." Reprinted in *Collected Poems,* p. 258.

133 The poet Herbert Palmer . . . Herbert Palmer, *Post-Victorian Poetry,* London, 1938, pp. 185–6.

PAGE

133   "with the Georgians . . ." "Poetry of Today," *Radio Times,* 2 November 1928, p. 290.

133   "is well done, certainly . . ." "The Future of the Novel," *Week-end Review,* 18 October 1930, p. 535.

133   Herbert Palmer remarks . . . Palmer, *op. cit.,* p. 212.

134   "He was thus . . ." "Wordsworth: Especially in Relation to Modern Poetry," *Essays by Divers Hands,* XXII (1945), 100.

134   One of the characteristics . . . For a brief analysis of the imagery in *The Garden,* see Stevens, *op. cit.,* pp. 34–40.

134   " 'April is the cruellest . . .' " *The Garden,* p. 63.

135   in a lecture . . . "Walter de la Mare and 'The Traveller,' " *Proceedings of the British Academy,* XXXIX (1953), 23–36 (Wharton Lecture).

135   in a radio tribute . . . "The Personality of Walter de la Mare," *Listener,* IL (30 April 1953), 711–12.

135   "He is far . . ." Wharton Lecture, *op. cit.,* p. 31.

135   "a question of focus . . ." "Some tendencies of Modern English Poetry," *Essays by Divers Hands,* VII (1927), 46.

135   "The Realists had . . ." Maurice Bowra, *The Heritage of Symbolism,* London, 1943, pp. 2–3.

136   "circumstantial detail . . ." "The Future of the Novel," *Week-end Review,* 18 October 1930, p. 535.

136   as we have already seen . . . *The Garden,* p. 89.

136   But as Maurice Bowra . . . Bowra, *op. cit.,* p. 220.

136   "a poet in a tradition" . . . Richard Church, "V. Sackville-West: A Poet in a Tradition," *Fortnightly,* CXLVIII (1940), 601.

136   "suffer from the delusion . . ." *Ibid.,* p. 604.

136   "A tired swimmer . . ." "Sissinghurst," reprinted in *Collected Poems,* pp. 111–12.

136   "a damned out-moded . . ." See Church, *op. cit.,* p. 607.

136   This awareness was . . . See above, p. 98.

137   "I had not read . . ." Interview published in *The Lady,* 6 June 1929, p. 771.

137   "He knows, he knows . . ." *The Garden,* p. 16.

137   "For who would bear . . ." *Hamlet,* III.i.

137   "another poet given . . ." Church, *op. cit.,* p. 601.

137   The subjective lyricism . . . They are the poems gathered under the headings "Love" and "King's Daughter" on pp. 283–325 of *Collected Poems.*

138   "Nec sum animi . . ." iii.289–90. "And well I know how hard it is to win with words a triumph herein, and thus to crown with glory a lowly theme" (Fairclough's translation in Loeb's Classical Library Series, Harvard, 1965). Dryden's translation, 1697, is:

> "Nor can I doubt what Oyl I must bestow,
> To raise my subject from a Ground so low:
> And the mean Matter which my Theme affords
> To embellish with Magnificence of Words."

138   "Through that restriction . . ." Church, *op. cit.,* p. 605.

PAGE

138   " 'the country habit . . .' " *The Land,* p. 5.

139   L. A. G. Strong recollects . . . "English Poetry Since Brooke," *The Nineteenth Century and After,* CXVI (1934), 464.

139   "Well, *I* can only say . . ." *Cassell's Weekly,* 19 March 1927.

139   *The Atlantic Book of British and American Poetry* . . . Pp. 832–36 (from *The Land,* pp. 50–57).

141   "There is no false . . ." Herbert Grierson and J. C. Smith, *A Critical History of English Poetry,* London, 1944, p. 505.

141   "During the war . . ." Letter dated 18 June 1971 from Richard Church.

141   "It is much more difficult . . ." *Diaries and Letters, 1939–45,* p. 265.

141   not yet been reprinted . . . Letter dated 26 November 1970 from Michael Joseph, Ltd.

141   "never stretching thought . . ." *Times Literary Supplement,* 15 June 1946, p. 285.

CONCLUSION

143   "a lack of interest . . ." *Diaries and Letters, 1945–62,* p. 38.

143   "neither do I feel . . ." Jacques Vallette, *Mercure de France,* 1-III-1949, in an unpublished letter he quotes on p. 427.

143   "I do get so frightfully . . ." *Diaries and Letters, 1945–62,* p. 38.

APPENDIX A

147   a memoir to Dyment . . . "Clifford Dyment: A Memoir," *Encounter,* August 1971, pp. 65–67.

APPENDIX B

150   "My son has gone . . ." Nigel Nicolson bought the Shiant Islands in the Outer Hebrides in 1937 (see *Diaries and Letters, 1930–39,* p. 288).

152   "Litany: I Am" There is a remarkable similarity between this poem and another, by Amergin, entitled "Song of Triumph," to be found in *Bards of the Gael and Gall,* ed. George Sigerson, London, 1907, pp. 110–11.

APPENDIX D

161   The earliest of these . . . A. L. Carvillon in *World's Work,* XLII (1923), 221–22, and J. Fletcher Smith in the Boston *Evening Transcript,* 18 August 1923.

161   They were followed . . . W. H. Chesson in *Bookman,* London (February 1924), 243–44.

161   After the award . . . See below, pp. 167–69.

161   in *Bookman* . . . New York, September 1930, pp. 21–26.

161   in *Canadian Forum.* 1931, pp. 462–63.

PAGE

161 in *La Stampa*. 5 December 1934, later reprinted in *Chronache Inglesi*, Milan, I (1950–52), 287–90.

161 in the *Fortnightly Review* . . . CXLVIII (1940), 601–8.

161 in *Eight for Immortality* . . . Dent, London, 1941.

161 in *Mercure de France* . . . 1-III-1949, pp. 423–31.

162 a German essay . . . *The Gate,* Bremen, II (1948), 3–6.

162 that by Richard Church . . . Poet, critic, author of *The Growth of the English Novel,* Oxford University Press, 1968.

162 Several of her books . . . Letters from V S-W's English publishers.

162 as *The Edwardians* is concerned . . . See above, p. 67.

162 80,000 copies . . . This figure is given in Doubleday, Doran's *Confidential Bulletin,* New York, 1 August 1931.

162 *The Land* is now in . . . Letter dated 17 September 1971 from William Heinemann Ltd. The letter adds, "A sale of over 50,000 copies of any book of poetry puts it in the best-seller class."

Bibliography

ARTICLES

"The lady of a tradition: Miss Sackville-West," Grant Overton, *American Nights Entertainment,* Appleton, New York, 1923, pp. 102–18.

"Victoria Sackville-West," S. P. B. Mais, *Some Modern Authors,* Richards, London, 1923, pp. 142–4.

"A novelist and her ancient heritage," J. Fletcher Smith, Boston *Evening Transcript,* 18 August 1923.

"A woman of letters," A. L. Carvillon, *World's Work,* XLII (August 1923), 221–2.

"V. Sackville-West," W. H. Chesson, *Bookman,* London, February 1924, pp. 243–4.

"Celebrities in undress: LXVIII—V. Sackville-West," Beverley Nichols, *Sketch,* 13 July 1927, p. 64.

"Victoria Sackville-West," H. J. Newbolt, *New Paths on Helicon,* Nelson, London, 1927, pp. 412–3.

"A woman of the day: V. Sackville-West," Winifred Holtby, *Yorkshire Post,* 19 August 1927, p. 6.

"V. Sackville-West," A. R. Marble, *A Study of the Modern Novel,* Appleton, New York, 1928, pp. 120–1.

"The Hon. V. Sackville-West," E. O. Hoppe, *Morning Post,* March 1929.

"Interviews with celebrities: The poet," Joan Grigsby, *Lady,* 6 June 1929.

"London literary letter," Hugh Walpole, *New York Herald Tribune,* 22 June 1930.

"V. Sackville-West," Hugh Walpole, *Bookman,* New York, September 1930, pp. 21–6.

"V. Sackville-West," ed. Louis Untermeyer, *Modern British Poetry,* Harcourt, New York, 1930, pp. 66–7.

"How writers work," Louise Morgan, *Everyman,* 23 October 1930, pp. 391–2.

"The new writers: XXI—Victoria Sackville-West," J. S. Will, *Canadian Forum* (1931), pp. 462–3.

"V. Sackville-West," S. J. Kunitz, *Living Authors,* Wilson, New York, 1931, pp. 353–5.

"Victoria Sackville-West: Ladies of Letters—I," Mary Craik, *Good Housekeeping,* February 1932, pp. 16–7, 108–9.

"Women Writers Today: Victoria Sackville-West—her exquisite mind and vision," Winifred Duke, *Glasgow Herald,* 27 September 1932.

"V. Sackville-West," Mario Praz, *La Stampa,* Rome, 5 December 1934. Reprinted in *Chronache Inglesi,* I (1950–2), Milan, 287–90.

"English Poetry Since Brooke," L.A.G. Strong, *The Nineteenth Century and After,* CXVI (1934), 460–8.

"V. Sackville-West: A poet in a tradition," Richard Church, *Fortnightly,* N.S., CXLVIII (1940), 601–8. Reprinted in Church, *Eight for Immortality,* Dent, London, 1941.

"Englische Dichterinnen I: Victoria Sackville-West," Hans B. Wagenseil, *The Gate,* Bremen, II (1948), 3–6.

"Victoria Sackville-West," Jacques Vallette, *Mercure de France,* 1–III–1949, pp. 423–31.

"V. Sackville-West," *Die Weltliteratur,* ed. E. Trauwallner, Wien, 1951, I, 444.

"V. Sackville-West," Stanley Kunitz, *Twentieth Century Authors,* 1st Suppl., Wilson, New York, 1955, p. 857.

"V. Sackville-West," *New Century Handbook of English Literature,* ed. Clarence Bernhart, Appleton-Century-Crofts, New York, 1956, p. 956.

"Full-length Portrait of Vita Sackville-West," Aileen Pippett, *Vogue,* CXXVIII (1956), 284–6, S 1.

"The Dismissal of Lord Sackville," C. S. Campbell, Jr., Biographical Footnotes, *Mississippi Valley Historical Review,* XLIV (March 1958), 635–48.

"George Osgoodby and the Murchison Letter," T. C. Hinckley, Biographical Footnotes, *Pacific Historical Review,* XXVII (27 November 1958), 359–70.

"V. Sackville-West," Franz Lennartz, *Ausländische Dichter und Schriftsteller unserer Zeit,* Kröner-Verlag, Stuttgart, 1960, pp. 589–91.

"V. Sackville-West," *Dizionario Universale della Letteratura Contemporanea,* ed. Mondadori, Milan, 1961, pp. 294–5.

"Språk och stil i två dikter av Victoria Sackville-West," Augusta Pierce (unpublished thesis), Stockholm, 1962.

"V. Sackville-West," *Lexikon der Weltliteratur,* ed. Gero von Wilpert, Stuttgart, 1963, I, 1161.

"The Reign of Louis XIV: A Select Bibliography of Writings Since the War of 1914–18," John B. Wolf, *Journal of Modern History,* XXXVI (March 1964), 127–44.

"V. Sackville-West," *Abriss der englischen Literaturgeschichte in Tabellen,* ed. Annemarie Schöne, Frankfurt a/M., 1965, pp. 267–8.

"V. Sackville-West," *Geschichte der englischen und amerikanischen Literatur,* ed. Walter F. Schirmer, 3. Aufl., 1966, II, 299–300.

"V. Sackville-West," *Der Romanführer,* Reklam-Verlag, Stuttgart, 1966, III, 214–6.

"V. Sackville-West," *Lexikon der Weltliteratur im 20. Jahrhundert,* Herder, Freiburg im Br., 1966, II, 831.

Anthony Burgess, *The Novel Now: A student's guide to contemporary fiction,* Faber & Faber, London, 1967, pp. 129–31.

"V. Sackville-West," Nancy MacKnight (unpublished thesis), Columbia University, New York, 1968.

"An Analysis of *The Garden* by V. Sackville-West," Michael Stevens (unpublished thesis), University of Uppsala, 1970.

"V. Sackville-West," *Meyers Handbuch über die Literatur,* 2. Aufl., Mannheim, 1970, p. 744.

"V. Sackville-West," *Dictionary of Literature in the English Language,* ed. Myers, Pergamon Press, Oxford, 1970, pp. 391, 745–6.

BOOKS

Altick, Richard D., *Lives and Letters: A History of Literary Biography in England and America,* Knopf, New York, 1965.

Bacquet, Paul, *Un contemporain d'Elisabeth I: Thomas Sackville*, Droz, Genève, 1966.

Bazin, Nancy T., *Virginia Woolf and the Androgynous Vision*, Rutgers University Press, New Brunswick, N.J., 1973.

Bell, Quentin, *Virginia Woolf*, Vols. I and II, Hogarth Press, London, Harcourt, Brace, Jovanovich, New York, 1972–73.

Blackstone, Bernard, *Virginia Woolf: A Commentary*, Harcourt, Brace, Jovanovich, New York, 1972.

Bowra, C. M., *The Heritage of Symbolism*, Macmillan, London, 1943 (Papermac 186).

Brewster, Dorothy, *Virginia Woolf*, Allen & Unwin, London, 1963.

Bullough, Geoffrey, *The Trend of Modern Poetry*, Oliver & Boyd, Edinburgh and London, 1949.

Burke's Peerage and Baronetage, London, 1970.

Calmette, Joseph, *Jeanne d'Arc*, Presses Universitaires de France, Paris, 1946.

Campbell, Roy, *The Georgiad*, Boriswood, London, 1931.

Complete Peerage, The, London, 1910–48.

Cordier, Jacques, *Jeanne d'Arc: sa personalité, son rôle*, Les Editions de la Table Ronde, Paris, 1948.

Cruse, Amy, *After the Victorians*, Allen & Unwin, London, 1938.

Dictionary of National Biography, The, London, 1885–1959.

Drew, Elizabeth A., *The Modern Novel*, Harcourt, Brace, New York, 1926.

Dunn, Waldo H., *English Biography*, Dent, London, 1916.

af Enehjelm, Helen, "En litterär vänskap: V. Sackville-West och *Orlando*," *Hemlängtan*, Medéns förlag, Stockholm, 1946.

Fabre, Lucien, *Jeanne d'Arc*, Tallandier, Paris, 1947.

Freedman, Ralph, "Virginia Woolf," *The Lyrical Novel*, Princeton University Press, New Jersey, 1963.

Garraty, John A., *The Nature of Biography*, Jonathan Cape, London, 1958.

Grierson, Herbert & Smith, J. C., *A Critical History of English Poetry*, Chatto & Windus, London, 1944.

Hafley, James, *The Glass Roof: Virginia Woolf as a Novelist*, University of California Press, Berkeley, Cal., 1954.

Hassall, Christopher, *Edward Marsh: A Biography*, Longmans, London, 1959.

Heilbrun, Carolyn, *Towards Androgyny: Aspects of Male and Female in Literature*, Knopf, New York, 1972, Gollancz, London, 1973.

Johnstone, J. K., *The Bloomsbury Group*, Secker & Warburg, London, 1954.

Lee, Sidney, *The Principles of English Biography* (Leslie Stephen Lecture), University Press, Cambridge, 1911.

Leslie, Anita, *The Marlborough House Set*, Doubleday, New York, 1973.

Marder, Herbert, *Feminism and Art*, University of Chicago Press, Chicago, 1968.

MacKnight, Nancy, "Vita: A Portrait of V. Sackville-West (doctoral dissertation), Columbia University, 1972.

McLaurin, A., *Virginia Woolf: The Echoes Enslaved*, Cambridge University Press, New York, 1973.

Nicolson, Harold, *Paul Verlaine*, Constable, London, 1921.

Nicolson, Harold, *The Development of English Biography*, Hogarth Press, London, 1927.

Nicolson, Harold, *Journey to Java*, Constable, London, 1957.

Nicolson, Harold, ed. Nigel Nicolson, *Diaries and Letters, 1930–39*, Collins, London, 1966.

Nicolson, Harold, ed. Nigel Nicolson, *Diaries and Letters, 1939–45*, Collins, London, 1967.

Nicolson, Harold, ed. Nigel Nicolson, *Diaries and Letters, 1945–62*, Collins, London, 1968.

Nicolson, Nigel, *Portrait of a Marriage*, Atheneum, New York, 1973.

Noble, Joan R., ed. *Recollections of Virginia Woolf*, Morrow, New York, 1972.

Palmer, Herbert, *Post-Victorian Poetry*, Dent, London, 1938.

Phillips, Charles, *History of the Sackville family, together with a description of Knole and the early owners of Knole*, Vols. I and II, Cassell, London, 1930.

Pippett, Aileen, *The Moth and the Star: A Biography of Virginia Woolf*, Little, Brown & Co., Boston, Mass., 1955.

Ross, Robert H., *The Georgian Revolt: Rise and Fall of a Poetic Ideal, 1910–22*, Southern Illinois University Press, Carbondale, 1965.

Sackville, Victoria Josefa, Lady, MS Diary, in the possession of Nigel Nicolson, Sissinghurst Castle, Kent.

Sackville-West, V., MS Autobiography, in the possession of Nigel Nicolson.

Sackville-West, V., MS Diary, in the possession of Nigel Nicolson.

Spender, Stephen, *World within World*, Hamish Hamilton, London, 1951.

Steegmuller, Francis, *La Grande Mademoiselle*, Hamish Hamilton, London, 1955.

Stevens, Michael, *V. Sackville-West: A Critical Biography*, Stockholm, January 1972, Michael Joseph, London, 1973.

Trautmann, Joanne, *The Jessamy Brides: The Friendship of Virginia Woolf and V. Sackville-West*, Penn State Studies, 1973.

Ward, A. C., *Twentieth Century Literature*, Methuen, London, 1945.

Watson, Sara Ruth, *V. Sackville-West*, Twayne English Authors Series No. 134, New York, 1972.

Wines, Jean, "A Bibliography of the Writings of Victoria Sackville-West," University of London, Dip. Lib., 1958.

Wolf, John B., *Louis XIV*, Gollancz, London, 1968.

Woolf, Leonard, *Downhill All the Way: An Autobiography of the Years 1919 to 1939*, Hogarth Press, London, 1967.

Woolf, Leonard, *The Journey not the Arrival Matters: An Autobiography of the Years 1939 to 1969*, Hogarth Press, London, 1969.

Woolf, Virginia, *Orlando*, Hogarth Press, London, 1928.

Woolf, Virginia, ed. Leonard Woolf, *A Writer's Diary*, Hogarth Press, London, 1954.

REVIEWS

The list makes no claim to completeness; it aims rather at providing a representative selection of reviews that have appeared in newspapers and magazines of repute, as well as those which have appeared in less well-known sources if they are of particular interest.

References are to the following newspapers and magazines:

A	*Archiv für das Studium der neueren Sprachen*, Braunschweig.	*BsM*	*Books of the Month*, London.
		BrE	*Brooklyn Eagle*.
		Bü	*Bücherei u. Bildung*, Bremen.
Ath	*Athena*, Berlin.	*BüW*	*Bücherwelt*, Hamburg.
AthL	*Athenaeum*, London.	*C*	*Cassell's Weekly*, London.
B	*Barke*, Frankfurt a/M.	*CH*	*Catholic Herald*, London.
BDM	*Birmingham Daily Mail*.	*ChT*	*Church Times*, London.
BI	*Bookfinder Illustrated*, London.	*CT*	*Catholic Times*, London.
BmL	*Bookman*, London.	*CoL*	*Country Life*, London.
BmN	*Bookman*, New York.	*DA*	*Dagstidningen Arbetaren*, Stockholm.
BRD	*Book Review Digest*, New York.		

DAG   Deutsche Allgemeine Zeitung, Ber-
      lin.
DN   Dagens Nyheter, Stockholm.
DNe   Daily News, London.
DT   Daily Telegraph, London.
E   Everyman, London.
ES   Evening Standard, London.
ET   Evening Transcript, Boston.
Fi   Figaro, Paris.
FNP   Frankfurter Neue Presse.
FR   Fortnightly Review, London.
FZ   Frankfurter Zeitung.
GH   Glasgow Herald.
Gr   Gral, München.
Gu   Guardian, London.
He   Heute, Berlin.
Ho   Hochland, München.
ILN   Illustrated London News.
It   l'Italia che scrive, Milan.
JC   Japan Weekly Chronicle, Yoko-
      hama.
JW   John O'London's Weekly.
L   Literarisches Zentralblatt für
      Deutschland, Leipzig.
LD   Literary Digest International
      Review, New York.
Lit   Literatur, Stuttgart.
Liv   Liverpool Daily Post.
LM   Mercury, London.
MaG   Manchester Guardian.
MdF   Mercure de France, Paris.
MP   Morning Post, London.
MPW   Morning Post, Würzburg.
NaL   Nation, London.
NaN   Nation, New York.
N&A   Nation and Athenaeum, London.
NeS   New Statesman, London.

NS&N New Statesman and Nation, Lon-
      don.
NL   Neue Literatur.
NoA   North American, Philadelphia.
NYH   New York Herald.
NYHT New York Herald Tribune.
NvB   Neues vom Büchermarkt.
Nw   Newsweek, New York.
NYT   New York Times.
NZZ   Neue Zürcher Zeitung.
Obs   Observer, London.
S   Saturday Review, London.
Sa   Saturday Review of Litera-
      ture, New York.
Sch   Schoolmaster, London.
Sco   Scotsman, Edinburgh.
SER   Scottish Educational Review,
      Edinburgh.
Sp   Spectator, London.
St   Star Telegram, Fort Worth,
      Texas.
SuT   Sunday Times, London.
SvD   Svenska Dagbladet, Stockholm.
SyD   Sydsvenska Dagbladet, Snällposten,
      Malmö.
SZ   Süddeutsche Zeitung, München.
Ta   Tagesspiegel, Berlin.
Ti   Times, London.
TLS   Times Literary Supplement, Lon-
      don.
WaS   Washington Star.
WD   Weekly Dispatch, London.
WdL   Welt der Literatur, Hamburg.
We   Welt, Hamburg.
Ww   Weltwoche, Zürich.
Ze   Zeit, Hamburg.
Zu   Zukunft.

Poems of West and East, MP, 12/10/17; *TLS*, 25/10/17.

Heritage, AthL, 30/5/19; *BmL*, June 1919; *BmN*, June 1919; *BrE*, 25/10/19; *ET*, 27/8/19;
    MdF, 15-VI-1920, p. 818; *MP*, 13/6/19; *NaL*, 14/6/19; *Obs*, 18/5/19; *Sco*, 19/5/19;
    SuT, 22/6/19; *TLS*, 22/5/19.

The Dragon in Shallow Waters, DNe, 12/7/21; *MdF*, 1-II-1922, p. 808; *NYH*, 13/10/21; *NYT*,
    26/3/22; *Obs*, 5/6/21; *Sp*, CXXVII (23/7/21), 115; *TLS*, 16/6/21.

Orchard and Vineyard, TLS, 1/12/21, p. 791.

The Heir, Bü, Mai—Juni 1949; *DT*, 11/8/22; *FNP*, 9/7/48; *NaN*, CIXX (3/9/24), 250;
    N&A, 24/6/22, p. 436; *LM*, 22/10/22; *Obs*, 18/6/22; *S*, 10/6/22; *Sp*, CXXVIII
    (24/6/22), 789; *Ta*, 2/8/48; *TLS*, 29/6/22, p. 427.

Knole and the Sackvilles, N&A, 6/1/23, p. 553; *Obs*, 17/12/22; *Sp*, (Lit. Suppl.) 10/2/23, p.
    218; *TLS*, 7/12/22, p. 809.

Challenge, NYT, 18/2/23, p. 11.

Grey Wethers, DT, 10/7/23; *N&A,* 28/7/23, p. 552; *NeS,* XXXIX (21/7/23), 448; *Sp,* 11/8/23, p. 197; *TLS,* 23/6/23, p. 438.

Seducers in Ecuador, Ath, Heft 4 (1947); *He,* 1/12/46; *MPW,* 4/4/47; *NYT,* 5/7/25; *TLS* 27/11/24, p. 794; *Zu,* 20/7/47.

The Land, BmL, LXXI (Nov. 1926), 112; *C,* 19/3/27; *MP,* 15/10/26, 17/6/27; *N&A,* XL (6/11/26), 188; *Obs,* Oct. 1926, Dec. 1926; *Sp,* 30/10/26, p. 758; *TLS,* 21/10/26, p. 716; *WD,* 30/1/27.

Passenger to Teheran, N&A, 4/12/26, p. 354; *Sp,* 11/12/26, p. 1081; *TLS,* 4/11/26, p. 758.

Aphra Behn, BmN, LXVII (June 1928), 445; *NaL,* CXXVII (5/9/28), 232; *N&A,* XLII (3/12/27), 360; *NeS* (3/12/27), 250; *NYHT,* 1/4/28, p. 7; *S,* CXLIV (26/11/27), 744; *Sp,* CXXXIX (12/11/27), 836; *TLS,* 24/11/27, p. 856.

Twelve Days, CoL, 10/11/28; *DT,* 9/11/28; *Sp,* CXLI (24/11/28), 781; *TLS,* Dec. 1928.

King's Daughter, BmN, LXXII (Feb. 1931), 649; *JC,* 5/12/29, p. 612; *Sp,* CXLIII (28/12/29), 984; *SuT,* 29/12/29.

Andrew Marvell, Obs, 19/1/30; *Sp,* CXLIII (21/12/29), 956; *TLS,* 17/10/29, p. 813.

The Edwardians, BmN, LXXII (Sept. 1930), 70—1; *BüW,* 29 J (1932), 148; *DN,* 18/11/31, p. 8; *Lit.* 34 J (1931—2), 293; *MaG,* 30/5/30; *NL,* XXXIV (Jan. 1933), 29; *NYT,* 7/9/30, p. 7; *Sa,* VII (13/9/30), 122; *Sp,* CXLVI (30/5/30), 872; *SvD,* 20/8/30; *TLS,* 29/5/30, p. 454.

Augustan Books of Poetry, Sch, 27/8/31.

Sissinghurst, E, 27/8/31; *MaG,* 27/8/31; *SER,* 20/11/31; *Ti,* 13/8/31; *TLS,* 21/9/33, p. 635.

All Passion Spent, BmN, LXXIV (Nov. 1931), 338; *FR,* CXXXVI (July 1931), 132; *Gr,* 26 J (1931—2), 293; *MaG,* 2/6/31; *NS&N,* I (6/6/31), 547; *NYT,* 30/8/31, p. 7; *Sa,* VIII (12/9/31), 116; *Sp,* CXLVI (30/5/31), 872; *St,* 20/9/31; *TLS,* 28/5/31, p. 424.

The Diary of Lady Anne Clifford, TLS, 1931.

Duineser Elegien, Sp, 21/11/31; *TLS,* 6/11/31.

Thirty Clocks Strike the Hour (The Death of Noble Godavary), BmL, July 1932; *Gr,* 27 J (1932—3), 451; *NYT,* 12/6/32; *Obs,* 10/7/32; *TLS,* 7/7/32, p. 501.

Family History, A, CLXV (1934), 305; *BmN,* LXXV (Nov. 1932), 734; *Gr,* 28 J (1933—4), 284—5; *MaG,* 28/10/32; *NS&N,* IV (22/10/32), 490; *NYT,* 30/10/32; *Sa,* IX (31/12/32), 353; *Sp,* CIL (22/10/32), 556; *TLS,* 13/10/32, p. 730.

Collected Poems, BDM, 11/12/33; *MaG,* 12/12/33; *NS&N,* VII (12/5/34), 740; *NYT,* 18/3/34, pp. 2, 15; *Obs,* 26/11/33; *TLS,* 30/11/33, p. 852.

The Dark Island, MaG, 2/11/34; *NS&N,* VIII (1/12/34), 794; *NYT,* 25/11/34, p. 6; *Sa,* XI (24/11/34), 309; *TLS,* 11/10/34, p. 692.

Saint Joan of Arc, BsM, June 1936; *ChT,* 1/6/36; *DN,* 19/7/36; *ES,* June 1936; *Ho,* 36 J, 338—41; *LD,* 88 J, 465; *Lit,* 39 J (1936—7), 572—3; *Liv,* 10/6/36; *MaG,* 10/7/36, p. 7; *MdF,* 1-IX-1936, p. 424; *NS&N,* XII (18/7/36), 96; *NYT,* 27/9/36, pp. 1, 18; *Obs,* 7/6/36; *Sco,* 11/6/36; *Sp,* CLVI (19/6/36), 1140; *SvD,* 16/10/37; *TLS,* 6/6/36, p. 469.

Pepita, DN, 10/11/38, p. 6; *Lit,* 41 J, 371—2; *MaG,* 2/11/37; *NS&N,* XIV (30/10/37), 695; *NYT,* 12/12/37, p. 9; *Obs,* 7/11/37, p. 11; *Sp,* 19/11/37, p. 24; *SuT,* 14/11/37; *SvD,* 13/11/38; *TLS,* 30/10/37, p. 796.

Solitude, NS&N, 24/10/38; *TLS,* 29/10/38, p. 690.

Selected Poems, TLS, 9/8/41, p. 387.

English Country Houses, TLS, 1/11/41, p. 546.

Grand Canyon, NYHT, 23/10/42; *NYT,* 25/10/42; *Obs,* 8/11/42; *TLS,* 7/11/42, p. 545.

The Eagle and the Dove, CH, 12/11/43, p. 3; *CT,* 31/12/43; *Gu,* 31/12/43; *JW,* 19/11/43; *MaG,* 17/11/43; *NS&N,* XXVI (13/11/43), 319; *NYHT,* 27/2/44; *NYT,* 20/2/44, pp. 3, 16; *Obs,* 26/12/43, p. 3; *Sp,* 19/11/43; *SuT,* 28/11/43; *TLS,* 11/12/43, p. 594.

Another World Than This, NS&N, XXX (15/12/45), 408; *SuT,* 2/12/45.

The Garden, MaG, 31/7/46; *NS&N,* 13/7/46, p. 32; *Obs,* 26/5/46; *Sp,* 31/5/46, p. 564; *TLS,* 15/6/46, p. 285.

Devil at Westease, It, XXXVIII (1955), 33; *NYT*, 11/5/47, p. 31.

Nursery Rhymes, DN, 24/4/51, p. 4; *TLS*, 4/10/47.

The Easter Party, DA, 11/12/54, p. 4; *DN*, 16/2/53, p. 2; *NS&N*, XLV (7/2/53); *NYT*, 15/2/53, p. 4; *Obs*, 25/1/53; *Sp*, CXC (6/2/53), 158; *SvD*, 16/3/53; *SyD*, 23/11/54, p. 8; *TLS*, 6/2/53, p. 88.

In Your Garden Again, TLS, 18/12/53, p. 820.

Daughter of France, MdF, Juillet 1959, p. 527; *NS&N*, LVII (18/4/59), 549; *NYT*, 30/8/59, pp. 7, 30; *NZZ*, 25/11/60; *Obs*, 5/4/59, p. 21; *ILN*,/CCXXXIV (1959), 704; *Sp*, 10/4/59, p. 518; *SyD*, 14/8/59, p. 4; *TLS*, 8/5/59, p. 267.

No Signposts in the Sea, B, II (1963), 52; *NvB*, II (1963), 16—7; *Nw* LVII (24/4/61), 66; *NS&N*, LXI (24/2/61), 313; *Obs*, 5/2/61, p. 28; *Sp*, 10/2/61, p. 198; *SZ*, 21/9/63; *TLS*, 10/2/61; *WeL*, 25/11/65; *Ww*, 1/4/66.

Faces: Profiles of Dogs, TLS, 22/12/61, p. 919.

Index